2001

THE EUROPEAN UNION

DILEMMAS IN WORLD POLITICS

Series Editor
George A. Lopez, University of Notre Dame

Dilemmas in World Politics offers teachers and students of international relations a series of quality books on critical issues, trends, and regions in international politics. Each text examines a "real world" dilemma and is structured to cover the historical, theoretical, practical, and projected dimensions of its subject.

THE
EUROPEAN UNION

■ ■ ■

Dilemmas of
Regional Integration

James A. Caporaso
University of Washington

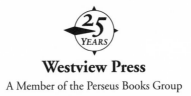

Westview Press
A Member of the Perseus Books Group

Copyright © 2000 by Westview Press, A Member of the Perseus Books Group

Published in 2000 in the United States of America by Westview Press, 5500 Central Avenue, Boulder, Colorado 80301-2877, and in the United Kingdom by Westview Press, 12 Hid's Copse Road, Cumnor Hill, Oxford OX2 9JJ

Find us on the World Wide Web at www.westviewpress.com

Library of Congress Cataloging-in-Publication Data
Caporaso, James A., 1941–
    The European Union : dilemmas of regional integration/James A. Caporaso.
        p.   cm.—(Dilemmas in world politics)
    Includes bibliographical references and index.
    ISBN 0-8133-2583-8 (pbk.)
    1. European Union.   I. Title.   II. Series.

JN30 .C38 2000
341.242'2—dc21   00-23372

The paper used in this publication meets the requirements of the American National Standard for Permanence of Paper for Printed Library Materials Z39.48-1984.

10   9   8   7   6   5   4   3   2

To Jeanice and Jody,
for your love and support throughout

□ □ □

Contents

□ □ □

Tables and Illustrations

□ □ □

Acknowledgments

In one sense everything we produce is social, the result of interconnected efforts of numerous people working together in recognized and unrecognized ways. This is even more so when it comes to writing a book. No one who writes a book can claim to be that parody of individualism, the "self-made man." I cannot imagine authoring a book without the support, criticism, and writings of others. The author may slave away during nights and weekends, but the raw materials he uses and the way he thinks about them are deeply affected by the environment within which he works. To claim authorship of an idea or point of view seems wrongheaded.

I would like to single out a few people to thank for their help. I was fortunate enough to have Joseph Jupille as a graduate student during the time I researched and wrote this book. Joe aided me with every part of the book: its design, the research, and the rewriting and elaboration of key points. He also read the manuscript in its entirety twice and prevented me from making mistakes. Finally, he introduced me to the wonders of the twenty-first century technology and the research possibilities afforded by this technology. I am now at least minimally equipped. I also want to thank Peter Dombrowski for reading the manuscript and making valuable comments thereon. Two other anonymous readers also provided extensive and helpful comments and criticisms which improved the manuscript. George Lopez has been very active providing leadership for the Dilemmas series. I thank him for his interest in the project and his helpful advice.

The teaching and research environments at the University of Washington have been very supportive. I have profited by teaching undergraduate courses on European integration for several years in a row. It is encouraging what can be accomplished in small classes with bright and curious students. Their enthusiasm for the subject matter never waned. There is nothing quite like teaching a course to galvanize one's thinking, to stimulate one to master the details of a complex subject, and to put it all in readable and perhaps even enjoyable form. To the extent I have succeeded, I owe much to my students. The research environment has also been quite supportive. I have been fortunate enough to hold the Virginia and Prentice Bloedel Chair for the past ten years. This chair has provided resources for research, travel, and summer support. I am especially indebted to my Vice-Provost Steven Olswang for his confidence in me and his generous support of my research. I also want to thank Yves Meny, Director of the Robert Schuman Centre of the European University Institute in Fiesole, Italy, for his support. The EUI hosted me during the 1996–1997 academic year, provided an office and computer, and access to its library. There could not have been a better environment in which to read, think, and engage in European studies.

Finally, I want to thank my wife Anne Grant Caporaso, my stepsons Jeff and David, and my daughters Jeanice and Jody, to whom this book is dedicated.

James A. Caporaso

□   □   □

Acronyms

ACP	countries of Africa, the Caribbean, and the Pacific
AMCHAM-EU	The EU Committee of the American Chamber of Commerce
APEC	Asia Pacific Economic Cooperation
ASEAN	Association of Southeast Asian Nations
CAP	common agricultural policy
CEECs	Central and Eastern European countries
CFSP	Common Foreign and Security Policy
CMEA (or Comecon)	Council for Mutual Economic Assistance
COPA	Committee of Professional Agricultural Organizations
CSCE	Conference on Security and Cooperation in Europe (became the OSCE in the mid-1990s)
DG	General Directorate
EC	European Community
ECB	European Central Bank
ECE	Economic Commission for Europe
ECJ	European Court of Justice
ECSC	European Coal and Steel Community
ECUs	European currency units
EEA	European Economic Area
EEC	European Economic Community
EFTA	European Free Trade Association
EMS	European Monetary System
EMU	Economic and Monetary Union
EP	European Parliament
EPC	European Political Cooperation
ERT	European Roundtable of Industrialists
ETUC	European Trade Union Confederation
EU	European Union
Euro	European currency
EUROCHAMBRES	Association of European Chambers of Commerce

GATT	General Agreement on Tariffs and Trade
GDP	gross domestic product
IGC	Intergovernmental Conference
IMF	International Monetary Fund
JHA	Justice and Home Affairs
LDCs	less developed countries
MEPs	members of the European Parliament
MERCOSUR	Southern Common Market
NAFTA	North American Free Trade Agreement
NATO	North Atlantic Treaty Organization
NGOs	non-governmental organizations
OPEC	Organization of Petroleum Exporting Countries
OSCE	Organization for Security and Cooperation in Europe
PHARE	Poland-Hungary Actions for Economic Reconstruction
PR	proportional representation
PTAs	preferential trade areas
QMV	qualified majority voting
SAP	Social Action Program
SEA	Single European Act
TEU	Treaty on European Union
UN	United Nations
UNICE	Union of Industries of the European Community
WTO	Warsaw Treaty Organization (Warsaw Pact)
WTO	World Trade Organization

ONE

□ □ □

Introduction

The term *paradox* is most closely associated with logic (Quine 1976) and conservative thought, while liberals rely on *dilemma* to convey much the same meaning. Marxists, when they wish to point to some tension within the economy or state, often use the stronger vocabulary of *contradiction*. Something in opposition, contrary, or out of place, seems to be conveyed by all three terms, but something different is hinted at too. It is not, as one often hears, "just" a question of semantics. The idea of paradox suggests a puzzle that is not yet fully thought through. The problem or inconsistency is there only because the analyst has not sufficiently thought through the premises. Thus, in rational choice theory, the paradox of voting (a paradox because the possibility of affecting the outcome is astonishingly small) is resolved when one discovers that people do not vote only to affect the outcome. Voting is an exercise in civic responsibility, and the act of voting is valued in itself, quite apart from its consequences. A liberal's world of tough trade-offs and dilemmas is much different. The choices between guns and butter, freedom and equality, and cosmopolitanism and community are not based on misunderstandings that can be corrected once we have done the analysis properly. Indeed, the very notion of choice logically implies that something must be given up.

Marxists, for their part, use the term contradiction to describe certain antagonistic features of capitalist society, on the assumption that these antagonisms are deeply ingrained and "structural," which is to say that they cannot be changed, short of revolution. Paradoxical thinking leads to further refinements to resolve anomalies, dilemmas urge us to develop clearer understanding of trade-offs and choices (including opportunity costs), and contradictions lead to radical thinking and action designed to change the structure of the system within which choices are made.

1

In this book I pursue the idea of dilemmas most seriously. The basic idea is simple, that many of the world's desirable and undesirable things are related to one another. When they are negatively related, it means that we can't get all of what we would like, and that the more we get of one good thing, the less we get of another. The metaphor of the horns of the dilemma[1] captures this trade-off nicely. To recognize a dilemma is merely to understand that not all good things go together. To pursue equality we may have to restrain the freedom of some members of society. To achieve a high level of readiness and security with regard to national defense, we will no doubt have to cut into spending for social welfare policies. To fully understand the nature of dilemmas, one must examine precisely the nature of the trade-offs; indeed, one must attempt to identify whether or not a trade-off exists. For example, for a long time most economists believed that there was a rather strong trade-off between deflation (price stability) and employment. The higher the level of employment, the less price stability one had. As more and more people took on jobs, and as the unemployment index went down to between 6 percent and 7 percent, the risks of inflation rose. However, in the United States in the late 1990s unemployment dipped to a low point between 4 percent and 5 percent, without causing any increase in inflation (indeed, inflation was extremely low by historical standards). Thus, something that was thought to be a dilemma was in fact not one.

It is not hard to find dilemmas at the level of regional integration in Western Europe. David Mitrany's article, written in 1930, titled "Pan-Europa: A Hope or a Danger?" suggested that a united Europe would present dangers just as it might also solve problems in other areas. Similarly, dilemmas could be suggested between the cosmopolitanism implied by regional integration and small-scale forms of association that go well with community, between efficiency on a regional scale versus equity (between regions and classes), between regional democracy and an elitism that focuses more on the accomplishment of specific tasks. The idea that trade-offs are involved is easy to accept. In some ways, there is a central trade-off that is presumed to be critical to the process of regional integration. This is the trade-off between national sovereignty and control on the one hand, and regional integration on the other. National sovereignty implies legal independence to decide on policies within a specific territorial area. Legal independence in turn implies the (exclusive) right to control one's borders, to decide on the fate of citizens within these borders, and to determine, ultimately, whether any external power should be listened to. Sovereignty, in short, is the ultimate right to decide. It involves the capacity to exclude external authorities (Krasner 1999, 4). As integration occurs, the emerging regional institutions acquire the ability to perform certain tasks, and with this ability comes pressure for legitimacy and the right to perform these tasks. If this occurs, that is, if regional institutions acquire the authority to perform specific tasks, then the authority of the constituent states is thereby diminished. The reality of this trade-off will be examined in many places throughout this book.

What are my goals in writing this book? I want, first of all, to write an accessible book, one that is readable by the novice as well as by those somewhat more advanced in knowledge of European affairs. The book is not simply a survey of the accomplishments of the European Union (EU), nor is it an effort to cover comprehensively all of the important issues of concern. This leads to my second goal, namely to focus on a set of important topics, and to deal with them in some detail, without feeling that I have shortchanged the reader by neglecting completely other topics. There are many books that provide overviews of the activities of the EU (see especially Nugent 1999; Dinan 1999). I choose to focus instead on three important areas from which the reader can profit by detailed examination. These three areas are social policy, democracy, and external relations. Of these three areas, the first two have not frequently been the central subject matter of books, while the last subject (external relations) has been extensively treated but not from the standpoint of many of the central dilemmas involved. Thirdly, since this is a book in a series of other books on dilemmas, I want to highlight some of the central dilemmas of the EU without at the same time ignoring the more harmonious areas of positive growth. Politics and economics are about collective gains (joint gains) as well as tough trade-offs.

Finally, I want to illuminate theoretical debates without making these same debates (over functionalism, federalism, intergovernmentalism) focal to the organization of the book, which implies that I occasionally refer to them. Periodically I use the key concepts that motivate these theories, without organizing the subject matter of the chapters around them.

THREE DILEMMAS OF EUROPEAN INTEGRATION

The three dilemmas central to this book relate to the construction of European social policy, to democracy or its absence at the European level, and to the thorny problems involved in the external relations of the EU. As a preview of the remainder of the book, I will briefly discuss each of these sets of dilemmas in the introduction. I turn to social policy first.

Social Policy, National or Supranational?

When the European Economic Community (EEC) came into existence in 1958, its major goals were stated in economic terms. The founding document of the EEC, the Rome Treaty, specified in detail the mechanics of achieving a free trade area and customs union. It also set forth goals, along with some concrete means to achieve them, for the formation of a common agricultural policy (CAP), common transport policy, common competition policy, and common market. It is not that all of these sectors enjoyed success quickly, or even at all (transport has shown little progress over the years). The point is simply that the overall goals of the EEC were predominantly economic, not political or ideological. As many have noted, the Rome Treaty provided a kind of economic constitution, a blue-print for the six original member states to follow to restore health to their economies. It suggested that countries should follow their comparative advantage, specializing in producing what they do best and then trade with others.

With this emphasis on economic efficiency, the EEC did not have much to say about social policy. Indeed, the social policy provisions were lim-ited to a handful of articles. With one exception (Article 119 on equal pay for equal work between men and women), these articles were very vague and more in the nature of a general statement of goals rather than con-crete programs of action. Further, the absence of a strong Treaty basis for progress on social policy was surely not an oversight. Social policies were very different from country to country, both in terms of the level of sup-port provided and in terms of underlying philosophy. In addition, the central theory of the functionalists who were so influential in getting the EEC off the ground (for example, Jean Monnet, Robert Schuman), ap-pealed to cooperation in areas of mutual benefit. Social policy, as an area of intense redistributional struggle, was not a likely candidate for early cooperation.

In line with the weak Treaty provisions, there was little actual progress in developing a common social policy. The main part of the energy of the EEC went to establishing a free trade area, customs union, and common market, though it was not until much later that the common market was established. Nevertheless, putting in place a common commercial entity and developing a common agricultural policy were the two primary tasks for the Community in the early years. Thus, it is no surprise that, by the time the Single European Act (SEA) was put into place in 1987, very little social policy had been agreed upon by the Commission and the Council of Ministers. However, as I will discuss in Chapter 2, the foundation of a European social policy has been laid, largely at the instigation of the Eu-ropean Court of Justice (ECJ).

The existence of a European social policy prompts us to explore two dilemmas in Chapter 2. The first one concerns the relation between na-tional social policies, already in place and usually very popular, and the aspiring European social policy. Is European social policy making any progress, and if so, are national policies being replaced by policies developed more comprehensively at the regional level? In general, do we see a competitive, even zero-sum, relationship between national and European social policies?

Second, given that social policy is advancing at the European level, we need to ask about its foundations. Two themes have organized our thinking about European social policy. The first theme links rights to the market. Market-driven conceptions of social policy see social policy as an accompaniment of market processes. The work of people in their daily economic lives creates practical situations that require governments to respond with social policy. The second theme sees rights as flowing from universal conceptions of citizenship, perhaps based on myths of common blood or membership in a historical community defined by a common territory.

People operating in a transnational market may lose work, become disabled, or choose to retire in a different country from the one in which they worked. A social policy may be justified solely in terms of its ability to make markets work better. A broader conception may see individuals as possessing social rights deriving from their citizenship in a political community. Rights may be thought of as universal within this community and not limited to market participation. So this second dilemma takes shape as a question about the way in which social policy is grounded, how it is justified. Is it ultimately justified by the market and are rights therefore limited by the extent to which individuals participate in the market, or do these rights have grounding in some conception of a European citizenship, tied to national citizenship but not identical to it?

Democracy Versus Markets, Democracy Versus Elitism

Chapter 3 devotes itself to the dilemmas surrounding democracy and European integration. The first task in this section is to clarify the meaning of democracy and to assess the democratic implications of European integration. A democratic system is generally taken to be one in which political institutions and rulers are responsive to the wishes of the public at large. The public, in turn, is one that is thought of as active and participant, rather than passive. Democracy requires something of its citizens as well as its rulers. The rulers must be listening and heeding the demands of the public, but the mass public must be proactive about communicating its demands. This abstract conception of democracy implies many things. It implies political competition among different would-be power holders. Democracy is arguably inconsistent with a system in which only one party is legal. A monopoly on political power would soon degenerate into corruption, self-aggrandizement, and unconcern about meeting the demands of the public. The public must be able to choose among different political programs. Democracy also implies representation, usually in the form of a legislature. There must be some organized way of conveying the preferences of individuals to those who make the laws. It also implies accountability of leaders and their practices which in turn rests on high levels of transparency, periodic elections, recall procedures, and so on. Finally, democracy implies a system of rights, that is, a set of guarantees that individuals cannot be deprived of certain basic things, such as personal freedom, free speech and association, the right to seek employment, the right to privacy, and so on.

There is no single definition of democracy even at the domestic level. A legislature and political parties are critically important to democracy in the United States, but parties are less important in France, where interest groups and parties are suspected of endangering the general will. Whereas multiple party systems exist in France, the Netherlands, Belgium, and Italy, two parties suffice in the United States and the United Kingdom; until recently one party has dominated Japanese politics.

When we transpose the definition of democracy to the European level, further complications arise, especially if we are looking for institutions that resemble those at the domestic level. There is a legislature—the European Parliament—but it does not closely resemble legislatures in the individual countries that make up the EU. Until recently, the EP has been quite weak and did not play a major role in making laws. However, from the original Rome Treaty to the present, the EP has progressively acquired new political powers. The Council of Ministers makes laws, in the sense that its agreement is required for any law to come into effect. However, the Council is composed of ministers from the individual states who are appointed by the national executives. Finally, there is the European Commission, a supranational bureaucracy that initiates legislation and oversees the implementation of the Treaty and secondary laws. The very independence of the Commission, which is often met with approval by proponents of European integration, keeps it from being on a tight leash with regard to democratically elected forces. As a result of all of these factors, the EU has often been criticized for its "democratic deficit" (Williams 1991).

Democracy at the EU level raises two distinct dilemmas. The first concerns the relation between democracy and the market. The second relates to democracy versus elitism. There are two received wisdoms concerning the relationship between democracy and the market. That first is that the two are not only compatible but that there is a strong affinity between them. This view is supported by a long-term historical connection between market capitalism and democracy as well as a number of subsidiary arguments. One argument is that markets facilitate (even demand) individual initiative and participation. Participation in markets prepares individuals for democratic participation at the same time that democratic individuality reinforces market behavior. A second argument is that markets imply economic decentralization, both of ownership (of private property, labor, capital) and allocative control. This decentralization is helpful in counterbalancing the tendency for political power to centralize. Dispersed economic power is necessary to preserve organized political competition.

Not everyone sees democracy and markets as so harmonious. There are several points of conflict. The first is that markets may override, corrode, and even destroy cherished values. Why does the French state have special laws to preserve small shops in cities, when the market would replace these shops with supermarkets? Similarly, Canadians and the French have argued that a free market puts everything up for sale, including a national culture. Thus, the state needs to play a role in defining the legitimate sphere of market exchange. In the EU this is a particularly salient issue, since the Single European Act set in motion a program to unify the European market by 1993, a project that was to a large extent successful. This enlarged market outpaced efforts to put in place laws and institutions to control it.

A second objection is that markets are not purely private. That is, they do not deal solely with exchanges that limit the costs and benefits to parties to the exchange. When a corporation comes into existence, and when it contracts to hire labor, dispose of capital, and make and sell products, it takes on a large public aspect. Corporations, as well as private individuals, are public in the straightforward sense that they "matter" for others. As such, their activities should be subject to public scrutiny and democratic control.

Since the central task of the EU has been to create a unified market, and since huge strides have been taken in this direction since 1958, the dilemma between the extension of the market and the strength of democratic procedures becomes more salient. Have democratic principles and practices been extended to the European level? How have national principles of elections, legislative oversight, party government, and judicial rights been extended (or not) to the European level?

External Relations

The significance of the EU is not limited to its internal development but also extends into the external realm. With the addition of Austria, Sweden, and Finland in January 1995, the EU has grown to over 375 million people and has a combined gross national product about 15 percent higher than the United States (Piening 1997, 4). It is also the largest commercial bloc in the world, accounting for just under 20 percent of world

FIGURE 1.1   Shares of World Trade, 1996

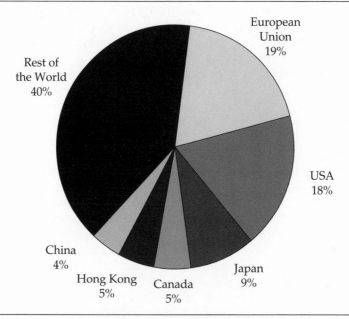

NOTE: Data for world trade exclude intra-EU trade.
SOURCE: Eurostat, *External and Intra-European Union Trade: Statistical Yearbook, 1958–1996* (Luxembourg: Office for Official Publications of the European Communities, 1997), pp. 26, 28.

trade (see Figure 1.1). A unit of this size and potential economic clout has to be taken into account by other countries. Even if the EU chooses a modest, low-profile foreign policy strategy, it is still difficult for it not to have a significant effect on other countries (see Figure 1.1).

From the very beginning, fears were raised about the relationship between regional integration in Europe and the outside world. The idea of "fortress Europe" was set against an open, liberal, cosmopolitan Europe interacting in a non-discriminatory way with the rest of the world. Similarly, there were those who suspected that an integrated Europe with a distinct regional identity would become a permanent state of affairs (Europe as an end-state) rather than a stepping stone or halfway house on the way toward a more comprehensive global integration.

These fears suggest a number of dilemmas that will be further explored in the chapter on external relations. The first dilemma asks whether the EU is a closed commercial state—the "fortress Europe" charge—or whether it is open and accommodating toward outsiders. Part of the answer to this question will be found in the commercial policy followed by the EU, the tariffs and other restrictions applied toward outsiders, and the relative differences in the obstacles to internal and external exchange.

In addition, the openness of the EU can be assessed by looking at the connections between regionalism and globalism. What is the role of the EU in the larger, global environment? Has it fostered or retarded broader cooperation? And how has the EU fared in global trade negotiations, under the General Agreement on Tariffs and Trade (GATT) and the World Trade Organization (WTO)? The final negotiations of the Uruguay Round witnessed some hard bargaining among the EU, the United States, and Japan. However, the results were arguably successful, judged by standards of global liberalization. Thus, the interplay between regional and global forces is not a settled matter.

A second dilemma of EU external development is captured by the "widening versus deepening" debate, which asks about whether the EU should "widen" to include new members, or "deepen" cooperation among existing members. With the end of the Cold War and the breakup of Yugoslavia, many new states, and some old ones too, have been set free to associate with other states as they choose. How many members should the EU take in? Its institutions were designed for a Community of six countries. The major concern is that, as the number of members increases, the strength of political institutions will decrease. The EU has expanded from the original six in 1958, to nine in 1973, to ten in 1981, to twelve in 1986, and to its current fifteen in 1995. Negotiations are currently under way with the Czech Republic, Poland, Hungary, Slovenia, and Estonia. In addition, Bulgaria, Latvia, Lithuania, Romania, and Slovakia are expected to begin negotiations sometime in the not-too-distant future, although they are not in the same fast-track category as the first five. Thus, sometime early in the next century, the EU could have as many as twenty-six members, making it quite a different body from the original six. Certainly, the institutions and rules designed for six countries may not serve as well for twenty-six.

A third dilemma concerns the attempts on the part of the member states to construct a Common Foreign and Security Policy (CFSP). Foreign policy cooperation poses the greatest difficulties and obstacles to cooperation. The stakes are likely to be high, the interests of member states divergent and conflictual, and the links to other members of the international system, especially the United States, very uneven. For all of these reasons, and because foreign policy and security are closely linked, nation-states are less likely to relinquish sovereignty in this area than in others. But in the absence of cooperation in foreign policy, states are less likely to have an impact. The dilemma, in short, is that if members do not cooperate, they will have minimal impact; if they do cooperate, they may be forced to relinquish some of their sovereign decisionmaking authority.

SUMMARY

A book organized around dilemmas commits itself to examine the tensions between many facets of the EU's economics and politics: between the original members and those left out; between labor and capital; between men and women; between elites and masses; and between the forces of the market and the rules designed to modify the market's operation. I have chosen to give in-depth accounts of three areas: social policy, democracy and its deficits, and external relations. Each is a broad area of concern with ample room inside to explore the difficult trade-offs that are inevitably part of the political process as well as the happier places where "all good things go together." The chapters ahead will provide the test of whether or not these goals have been achieved.

NOTES

1. The term "dilemma" actually refers to a situation in which one is confronted with two alternatives, both of which are equally unfavorable. Such a situation does not present a choice at all since the person is indifferent to the outcome. See *Oxford Universal Dictionary*, third edition, Rand McNally and Co., 1955.

2. For an excellent treatment of external relations, see Piening 1997.

REFERENCES

Dinan, Desmond. 1999. *Ever Closer Union: An Introduction to European Integration*, 2nd ed. Boulder, Colo.: Lynne Rienner Publishers.

Krasner, Stephen D. 1999. *Sovereignty: Organized Hypocrisy*. Princeton, N.J.: Princeton University Press.

Mitrany, David. 1930. "Pan-Europa: A Hope or a Danger?" *The Political Quarterly* 1, no. 4 (September-December): 457-478.

Nugent, Neill. 1999. *The Government and Politics of the European Union*, 4th ed. London: Macmillan.

Piening, Christopher. 1997. *Global Europe: The European Union in World Affairs*. Boulder, Colo.: Lynne Rienner Publishers.

Quine, W.V. 1976. *The Ways of Paradox, and Other Essays*. Cambridge, Mass.: Harvard University Press.

Williams, Shirley. 1991. "Sovereignty and Accountability in the European Community." In *The New European Community: Decisionmaking and Institutional Change* edited by Robert O. Keohane and Stanley Hoffmann. Boulder, Colo.: Westview Press.

TWO

□   □   □

European Social Policy:
National or Regional?

Judging from the content of the Rome Treaty, which is primarily an economic document, the founders of the European Economic Community (EEC) did not foresee a comprehensive social policy developing at the European level. There are many reasons for this. While many of the member states were highly interventionist and *dirigiste* (centrally directed) regarding their own economies, the move to the European level was seen in less interventionist terms, that is, as involving the freeing up of the market. Second, welfare states, with which social policy is tightly associated, were then and remain highly popular with the electorate. It is not likely that national politicians would willingly transfer policymaking competence for social policy to the European level. Indeed, pressure to do so did not exist. Third, the anticipated success of the EEC rested to a large extent on the ability of leaders to steer clear of the shoals of redistributional politics (see Box 2.1). Because the EEC did not have broad support, and did not enjoy the legitimacy of the voters in the member states, it was thought best to concentrate on relatively depoliticized, technical matters such as trade, health and safety and so on. These areas provided the prospects of collective gains and thus avoided the divisive aspects associated with redistribution.

Thus, when the EEC came into operation in 1958, the member states sought to establish a common market, comprising a common external tariff and internal free movement of goods, services, and productive factors. A common market is one of the five levels of economic integration identified by Balassa (see Table 2.1)

> In a free trade area, tariffs (and quantitative restrictions) between the participating countries are abolished, but each country retains its own tariffs

11

Box 2.1 Redistributional Politics

Politics is redistributional when it involves taking wealth from some and transferring it to others. This type of political activity is inherently conflictual in relation to what might be called efficiency politics, which involves government programs to better the lot of society as a whole (for example, clean air, defense, infrastructure). Examples of redistributional politics include public expenditures to support advanced educational degrees, grain price supports, unemployment insurance, and research and development spending for advanced aircraft. In all of these cases, money is "taken" from some (often in the form of taxes) and transferred to others in the form of subsidies, tax incentives, and so forth.

against non-members. The establishment of a customs union involves, besides the suppression of discrimination in the field of commodity movements within the union, the creation of a common tariff wall against nonmember countries. A higher form of economic integration is attained in a common market, where not only trade restrictions but also restrictions on factor movements are abolished. An economic union, as distinct from a common market, combines the removal of restrictions on commodity and factor movements with a degree of harmonization of economic, monetary, fiscal, social, and countercyclical policies. Finally, total economic integration presupposes the unification of economic, fiscal, etc. policies and requires the setting up of a supranational authority whose decisions are binding for the member states (Balassa 1961, 5–6).

Member states agreed upon a twelve-year transition period (1958–1970) during which time tariffs and quantitative restrictions on goods and services were to be eliminated. The six original members (Belgium, France, Germany, Italy, Luxembourg, and the Netherlands) succeeded in reaching this goal a year and a half ahead of schedule, by July 1, 1968. However, the same success for setting up a common market for labor and capital proved more elusive. Labor and capital posed special problems. People in different countries could easily trade machinery, food, and consumer electronics goods. Economic exchange of this type simply enlarged the scope of consumer choice. But an integrated, region-wide market for labor raised problems not encountered with the movement of goods and services. For workers to move freely across countries,

TABLE 2.1   Forms of Economic Integration

	Free Movement of Goods	Common External Tariff	Free Movement of Factors	Monetary, Social, and Macroeconomic Policy Harmonization	Unified Economic, Fiscal, Social Policies and Binding Supranational Authority
Free Trade Area	X				
Customs Union	X	X			
Common Market	X	X	X		
Economic Union	X	X	X	X	
Total Economic Integration	X	X	X	X	X

SOURCE: Derived from Balassa 1961, 4–5.

member states had to agree on the mutual recognition of credentials as certified by other countries. For example, hairdressers, electricians, plumbers, chefs, doctors, and architects all enter a period of training and receive certification in their home countries. Often the criteria that define certification differ across countries. Obviously, these criteria would either have to be harmonized, or some sort of agreement would have to be reached regarding the acceptance of differences in national standards. In addition, differences in social security schemes would have to be taken into account. A worker might work five years in the Netherlands, ten in Germany, and four in Italy and meet the minimum standards for social security payments in none of them. Unless this situation were addressed, it would provide an obvious obstacle to the movement of workers. The same is true for the movement of capital. If countries have laws that limit investment in certain industries to domestic firms and individuals, or limit capital outflows, there can be no common market in capital. A common market for capital requires open stock exchanges, freedom to trade financial services (that is, to shop for loans in different countries), and a willingness to allow corporations from foreign countries to set up shop within a nation's borders. Many countries have been reluctant to do these things.

Thus it is not surprising that a full common market for labor and capital did not arrive until much later than the free trade area and customs union. The entry into force of the Single European Act (SEA) in 1987, and the associated "1992 Program," were the means used to create a truly unified market by the end of 1992. Taken together, the creation of a free trade area (no internal tariffs) and customs union (common external tariff toward nonmembers) on the one hand, and the unification of labor and capital markets on the other, have made substantial progress toward creating a European market.

Many people have pointed out that the European Union is primarily an economic project. To a certain extent this is true. The European project has not centered on building a unified supra-state modeled on the existing nation-states. The EU does not have a military, does not provide for the common defense, has only minimal provisions for European citizenship, and possesses only the beginnings of a social policy. Yet, much of what the EU originally intended to do was accomplished by 1993. While a unified market existed, it was difficult to think of a European state.

Markets, however, do not exist by themselves. They are embedded in society as a whole. Bankers, employers, managers, and workers produce, distribute, buy and sell, save, invest, and consume. While economic analysis focuses on these activities, it is useful to keep in mind that people in their economic capacity are also active in other ways. They are connected to families, churches, militaries, friends, professional institutions, interest groups and so on. When a worker loses a job, or a firm is forced out of business, the implications extend beyond the economic realm. People are put out of work, lose their property (including capital), income, means of consumption, status, and often self-esteem. Because of these disruptions, governments at the national level have developed numerous programs to support, retrain, and in general protect individuals from adverse market effects. Such programs include housing, energy allowances, maternity leave support, unemployment insurance, old-age insurance, medical assistance, student scholarships, and retraining grants.

The types of programs mentioned above were developed by national governments beginning in the nineteenth century and have continued up to the present. Collectively they go by the name "social policy." The type of state structure associated with these social policies is the modern welfare state. Since national states presently control welfare policy, it might seem odd to devote a chapter to the European dimensions of social welfare policy. Yet the development of a region-wide market prompts the question: "What about the social aspects of economic activity at the European level?" Does the European Union, despite the strong association between social policy provisions and national governments, manage to develop a European layer of social policy? How does European social policy affect the policies and sovereign status of the member states?

The key dilemma addressed in this chapter lies in the struggle between national control over social policy and the demands at the regional level for social policy to address the concerns of the unified market.

SOCIAL POLICY

The modern welfare state took shape during the last two decades of the nineteenth century and the 1920s. During this time, pension and social security programs were established for workers and needy citizens in Europe. These programs laid the foundations that were later expanded into other areas marked by more comprehensive income support and social insurance. The expansion of social policy in the United States came much later, during the New Deal of the thirties, though some policies existed earlier (Skocpol 1995, 11–12).

Given the wide array of social policies in different countries, a definition would be useful. T. H. Marshall's classic definition of social policy is the use of "political power to supersede, supplement, or modify operations of the economic system in order to achieve results which the economic system would not achieve on its own" (Marshall 1975, 15). Thus, social policy refers to government activity and laws designed to secure a variety of normative social objectives, such as aid to the poor, minimum income, childcare allowances, and the retraining of workers. Each of these objectives could be reinterpreted in self-interested terms, that is, minimum income programs could be seen in Counter-cyclical terms, as demand-management. (Counter-cyclical policy involves the use of government resources to counter the dominant economic trend. The government spends more when economic growth is slow and restricts the supply of money when the economy is "overheated.") However, social policy also implies that there is some normative content to the program at issue. This comes out most clearly in regard to child labor laws, laws to protect the elderly, the blind, the sick and unfortunate and so on.

While social policy refers to policies designed to achieve social objectives not realized by the market, the market generally serves as the starting point for discussion of social policy. The market's chief claim to our loyalty is that it is the most efficient way to organize our economic activities. At the most basic level, a market is a social institution for buying and selling. It is a mechanism to facilitate economic exchange of goods, services, and productive factors. Markets today are global in scope. However, if we want to understand the foundations of a market, we are not led far astray if we think of a market as "our local market," say an open-air market where food, dry goods, clothing, and jewelry are sold. In this exchange system, people will buy and sell, that is, they will part with their money or their goods, in exchange for things they want more. This process of exchange will take place until there are no more goods available for which there are buyers with both wants and money. At this point, the market is in equilibrium.

Many economists argue that the market is the most efficient arrangement for satisfying wants. At some level, everyone owns something, whether it is money, land, one's own labor, special knowledge, or finished goods. The market facilitates the rearrangement of property according to the wants and resources of its owners (Caporaso and Levine 1992, 38–39). At that point, the market has accomplished its social purpose. However, even when markets work well they do not assure all social objectives. Far from it. They do not provide security, guarantee jobs or income, satisfy the wants of the needy, nurture feelings of community, produce public goods such as defense, or control externalities such as pollution. To say this is not to provide a critique of markets so much as to recognize their limitations. Markets "provide" primarily for those who actively partici-pate. Participation requires assets. In economics the term "demand" does not signify what I as an individual want or need. Rather it means that a want is backed up with money resources to purchase certain goods. Mar-kets do not automatically care for the sick, needy, very young and old, the disabled, and unfortunate. This is where social policy enters. Through so-cial policy, governments try to realize numerous policy objectives not available through the market.

SOCIAL POLICY DILEMMAS

Historically, the development and control of social policy have been the province of nation-states. The explosive expansion of social programs in advanced capitalist democracies during the twentieth century has been a national phenomenon in the sense that nation-states have controlled the pace and nature of change. While welfare states share many similarities, there are also important differences in scope and style, especially if one contrasts the United States, Japan, and Western Europe.

Even within Europe, there are important differences between north and south, and between continental welfare states and Great Britain. Greece, Portugal, and Spain spend very little on social programs whereas Den-mark, Germany, and Luxembourg spend quite a lot (see Figure 2.1). Some countries tie payment of services to locale (for example, British agencies pay for medical services rendered in Great Britain, and monies come out of the British public Treasury); others determine payment by the citizen-ship of the patient in question. National attitudes about the scope of the market, social responsibility for unemployment, and the limits of state in-tervention for illness, pregnancy, child-rearing, and old-age insurance are products of distinctive national goals and histories, and expenditures for these functions vary meaningfully across EU member states (see Table 2.2). Yet, the creation of a transnational market generates pressures for so-cial coordination and social policy. To see how the regional market gener-ates demands for coordinated social policy, consider the following exam-

Figure 2.1   Social Expenditures per Capita, 1994

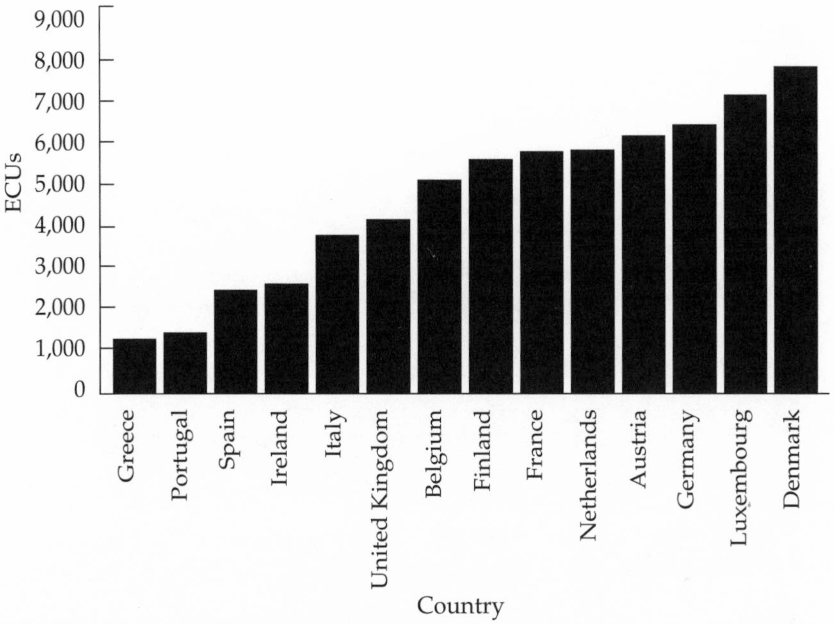

NOTE: Data for Sweden not available.
SOURCE: Eurostat, *Basic Statistics of the European Union,* 33rd edition
(Luxembourg: OOPEC, 1996), p. 169.

ples. Suppose a Danish couple retires to Portugal and one of them requires an operation and hospital stay in Portugal. Who pays for the medical service, the country where the service takes place, or the country
where the patient has citizenship? Suppose an Italian worker in Munich is
fired or loses employment due to an accident on the job. Is he/she eligible
for German unemployment or disability insurance? Suppose that the children of Spanish workers in France want to go to college in their home
country, that is, in Spain. Is the free education to which the child is entitled in France also good for a college education in Spain?

These examples serve to illustrate the kinds of complications that are
encountered whenever individuals cross national frontiers to take up employment in another country. While these complications raise normative
issues about the "right" policy to follow in particular circumstances, they
can also be viewed from the standpoint of economic efficiency. If issues
relating to the recognition of credentials, unemployment insurance, pensions, and the like are not dealt with at the European level, this consti-

TABLE 2.2 Social Protection Benefits by Function (% total benefits), 1994

	Unemployment	Disability	Sickness and Health Care	Old Age and Survivors	Family and Children	Miscellaneous
Belgium	15.3	7.0	26.8	40.0	8.8	2.1
Denmark	16.3	10.0	17.6	37.0	12.3	6.7
Germany	12.4	6.7	29.2	41.7	7.3	2.8
Greece	NA	NA	NA	NA	NA	NA
Spain	18.4	13.6	28.4	37.5	1.4	0.7
France	8.2	5.7	29.0	43.4	9.0	4.7
Ireland	16.9	4.4	34.3	27.6	11.7	5.1
Italy	2.3	7.5	22.4	64.3	3.6	0.0
Luxembourg	2.3	13.7	24.6	46.0	13.3	0.2
Netherlands	10.8	15.5	28.8	36.7	4.8	3.4
Austria	6.6	7.1	24.0	47.2	13.5	1.5
Portugal	5.5	14.1	34.5	39.8	5.6	0.4
Finland	15.6	14.8	20.6	31.9	13.6	3.5
Sweden	11.7	11.5	21.4	36.9	11.9	6.6
United Kingdom	6.6	11.7	25.6	39.3	8.9	7.9

SOURCE: *Eurostat Yearbook '97: A Statistical Eye on Europe, 1986–1996* (Luxembourg: OOPEC, 1997), pp. 246–247.

tutes a serious obstacle to the mobility of labor, which in turn would reduce economic efficiency.

The EU is made up of fifteen countries comprising a single market. Yet,
Europe is not similarly unified at the level of culture and political institutions. Each country has a distinct and largely sovereign political system.
Each is made up of at least one dominant culture. The tension between an
integrated European-level market and a largely decentralized political
system of national states poses several interesting dilemmas. The first
dilemma relates to national versus regional (or supranational) social policy provisions. What is the emerging shape of social policy in Europe as a
whole? Have significant advances in social policy taken place at the European level, or has control of social policy remained firmly in the hands of
member states? As social policy becomes more Europeanized, will this
process take place at the expense of member states? Does the appearance
of a European social policy displace or compete with national policy or is
it more accurately viewed as another policy layer grafted on top of national policies.

These questions raise concerns closely tied up with national sovereignty in at least two senses. First, sovereignty implies the ultimate right
to decide. That is, within every society, there must be some institution
where decisions are made that cannot be legally contradicted by any
other institution in that society. Such a view of sovereignty implies a hierarchy of norms in which national laws clearly trump international and
sub-national laws. Second, the idea of sovereignty implies the ability to
exclude "external" authorities, and external authority claims (Krasner
1999). Indeed, this second view of sovereignty is at least partly implied by
the first. If an institution, say the British Parliament, has the ultimate right
to decide, then it cannot also be true that some external authority, say the
Pope or the United States Congress, also has the ultimate right to decide.
In this sense, sovereignty structures are exclusive, at least with regard to
any particular issue. Thus, when we ask about the locus of policymaking
in social affairs, we are also asking about the level of government which
has responsibility for social affairs, national or supranational, or both.

The second dilemma identifies a tension between two different conceptions of social policy, one based on the market and the other on citizenship. The first conception sees social policy as closely linked to, and ultimately legitimated by, the market. For individuals to be able to take
advantage of social policy at the European level, they would first of all
have to participate in the European market. In addition, they would have
to be eligible in some way, either through unemployment provisions, job
training, sickness, old age insurance, dependency allowances and so on.
As broad as this conception is, it nevertheless remains tethered to market
participation. Social policy refers to the sum total of policy adaptations

made in response to and in anticipation of free movement of workers, capital goods, and services.

The second conception of social policy moves beyond markets to a more rights-based idea flowing from citizenship not necessarily tied to markets. For example, child abuse and family violence have no necessary and direct connection to the market but could become the subjects of legislation under a broad conception of citizenship. In this broader conception of citizenship, social policy could be determined on the basis of various criteria—need, merit, or inclusion in a political community, the political community constituted by the EU itself. Thus, to be a European citizen implies that one is entitled to certain benefits, as well as bound by certain obligations. But citizenship constructed along these lines begs the very question about whether a European political system exists. Traditional conceptions of citizenship equate being a citizen with being a member of the *polis* or state. The German word for citizenship, *Staatsangehoerigkeit*, captures this traditional meaning. Literally translated, it means belonging to a state.

I close this section with some comments on the relationship between markets and citizenship. Once again, it is best to think of markets as large-scale institutions of economic exchange, connecting producers and consumers, buyers and sellers, workers and capitalists and so on. The market has progressively moved from a national to a regional and global scale, connecting individuals, firms, and banks across the fifteen member states. Indeed, when the EU's Economic and Monetary Union (EMU) came into effect in January 1999, it introduced a single currency (the Euro) and created a European Central Bank (ECB). The EU thus had a single currency to complement its single market. Judged against this economically integrated market, social policy is hopelessly fragmented among fifteen different countries. For the most part, social policy rights, as citizenship rights in general, are exercised within established national states. Thus, to be French, British, or Italian implies certain rights and obligations, similar in some respects to be sure but different in important ways too. Yet the new regional economic level implies a new set of problems, arising out of the operation of a unified market. What happens when these problems (for example, unemployment of migrant workers, medical services for nationals of other member states) appear at the regional level, within a space that is not the exclusive preserve or responsibility of any particular country? Are they ignored? Are they dealt with individually, ignoring the externalities for other countries? Or do the member states work out some system of coordinated response? I return to these questions below.

In the following sections, I explore some of the developments in the area of social policy in the European Union. First, I give a brief review of social policy proposals and activities in order to place the role of the Council of Ministers and Commission in context. Success at this level remains limited. Second, I move to the less studied, but in many ways more important, activities of the European Court of Justice (ECJ) in social policy. Then I return to the two dilemmas, examining them once more in light of the evidence.

A BRIEF HISTORY OF EU SOCIAL POLICY

Architects of the European Community doubtless had many goals in mind. Visions of peace, economic progress, and social harmony were prominent in the minds and writings of those who argued on behalf of a United Europe. The organization and implementation of the Marshall Plan (1947), as well as the creation of the European Coal and Steel Community (ECSC, 1952) and European Economic Community (EEC, 1958), reflected desires for international cooperation, domestic social harmony, as well as economic prosperity. In addition, there is an important sense in which the creation of the EEC was premised on a loss of confidence in the nation-state system. The organization of the European world into nation-states, competing with one another according to the logic of the balance of power system, had produced two major world wars in the twentieth century and the loss of lives of millions of citizens. There was a belief, prominent among some statesmen and intellectuals, that the excesses of nationalism had to be held in check. The creation of the ECSC and later the EEC provided an institutional framework for doing just that.

Despite the appeal of creating an international organization that went "beyond the nation-state," the hard core of the EEC was, as implied by its name, economic. The central purposes, through which other aims were to be facilitated, were economic: the creation of a regional free-trade zone and customs union, the destruction of cartels, efforts to increase the efficiency of the agricultural sector, and the deepening of the regional division of labor. Regional integration was to promote efficiency, competition, and wealth. This increased wealth would soften the divisions among classes and groups and promote an environment within which political compromises could be achieved.

Compared to the economic content of the Treaty of Rome, the provisions related to social policy were modest. Articles 117–122 of the original treaty set out the general goals of the member states in social policy. However, with the exception of Article 119 on equal pay for equal work, the goals are just that—general statements of purpose—rather than concrete guidelines for states to follow. Article 117 recognized the "need" to "promote improved working conditions and an improved standard of living for workers." Article 118 entrusted the member states with the task of "promoting close cooperation in the social field." Articles 120–122 dealt with maintaining equivalence of paid holidays, social security of migrant workers, and provisions for reporting social policy developments in the Commission's annual report to the European Parliament.

Few would argue that these six articles constituted a bold, dramatic, and comprehensive program to develop a European social policy. More realistically these Treaty provisions attempted to provide the basis, conceptual as well as legal, for extending domestic social policy to the European level, in order to cover cases not adequately dealt with domestically, or to respond to complications arising from the transnational market. With capital and labor crossing national lines at unprecedented rates, new problems were bound to emerge, for example, social security benefits, sick leave, maternity care, and student scholarships. In the case of such conflicts, which principles were to govern? Did place of work or country of citizenship count more?

Regarding the general nature of Articles 117–122 (as well as 123–128 on the European Social Fund), Article 119 was something of an exception. Article 119 stated that "Each member state shall during the first stage ensure and subsequently maintain the application of the principle that men and women should receive equal pay for equal work." While the phrases "equal pay" and "equal work" are not without ambiguities, the injunction here is straightforward. If men and women are doing the same work, they should be paid equally. There should not be separate pay scales for men and women.

The reasons for the specific nature of Article 119 are interesting. They did not have to do with a breakthrough in abstract conceptions of gender equality in the late 1950s. Instead, Article 119 was included largely at French insistence. French law already required equal pay for men and women. This legislation went back to the end of World War II at which time France experienced severe labor shortages. Women were to alleviate the labor shortages by participating in the market. Parts of the French Resistance movement, particularly the Left, felt strongly about achieving greater social equality, partly for its own merits and partly because higher pay for women meant the reduction of family poverty. Although women had barely achieved the vote by the end of the War, their activism and participation in the post-war strikes and bread riots of 1946–1947 increased their political clout (Hoskyns 1996, 54). To encourage women to take on wage work, the French constitution of 1946 and subsequent domestic laws sought to protect against wage discrimination between men and women. In order to protect their domestic market and to prevent unfair competition, France argued for the transposition of their gender equality law to the European level. Regardless of the intent, however, the

European Court of Justice would make good use of this provision to create a jurisprudence centering on gender equality in the marketplace.

Social policy was not one of the first areas to demonstrate progress in the EEC. This is hardly surprising. The EEC was not intended to be a supranational state with massive powers to tax and spend across national borders. The 1956 Spaak Report (after Paul Henri Spaak) that laid the basis for the negotiations leading to the Treaty of Rome argued that "redistributive benefits used as instruments of social policy should remain entirely a matter for states" (Hoskyns 1996, 48). The first twelve years (1958–1970) were preoccupied with establishing the free trade area, customs union, and common agricultural policy (CAP), and very little happened in social policy.

The leaders of the member states periodically tried to get the ball rolling, but for the most part it was to no avail. At the Paris Summit meeting of 1972 the Heads of State or Government issued a communiqué stating that they attached as much importance to vigorous action in the social field as to the achievement of economic and monetary union (*Bull. EC* 10 1972: 19). Events of the late 1980s belied this rhetoric, providing dramatic progress in the EMU accompanied only by a lofty but unenforceable declaration of the "fundamental social rights of workers." The 1972 Summit had been called by Georges Pompidou of France and was intended to mark the relaunching of Europe. The agenda and the outcomes were orchestrated by Pompidou (France), Brandt (Germany), and Heath (Great Britain) (Hoskyns 1996, 80). However, few concrete steps were taken to translate lofty pronouncements into policy!

As a result of this meeting, the Commission was instructed to produce a Social Action Program (SAP), including suggestions of practical measures to achieve the objectives laid down. The Commission came up with the first such program in 1974. The document was wide-ranging and addressed itself to the issues of full employment, living and working conditions, worker participation in industrial decisionmaking, and equal treatment of men and women (Dinan 1994, 396).

While the first SAP is not usually judged a success, two important developments should be noted. First, it did produce some legislative successes. Among these were a directive on collective firings, one on worker's rights in the case of business delocation, and one on the protection of salaried employees when their employers become insolvent (Dutheillet de Lamothe 1993, 197). Most notably for our purposes, two important Directives were passed in 1975 and 1976 relating to gender equality in the market. The Equal Pay Directive (1975) and the Equal Treatment Directive (1976) were extremely important in that they set the stage for subsequent litigation on behalf of citizens (usually women) in the member states. The Equal Pay Directive identified a matter of some contention among the member countries. For strong defenders of the market, pay is simply a return to labor in accordance with market principles of supply, demand, and productivity. Wages are therefore set in the private sector in a process that involves employer, workers, and the market. Countries disagreed on the proper amount of government intervention to use to bring about equal pay, even if they agreed that men and women should be paid equally in principle.

At various stages of the negotiations for this Directive, the German, Danish, and British delegations were opposed to its passage, which would require harmonization of the national laws of all the member states (Hoskyns 1996, 88). The main source of the disagreement had to do with inclusion of the phrase "or work for equal value." In other words, the equal pay provisions were to apply not only to the same (identical) work but also to "like work" or "comparable work." In the end, only the British held out and even they signed a modified text ("work to which equal value is attributed") in the expectation that their own national legislation—the Equal Pay Act of 1975—would be consistent with the European standard. As it turned out later, the British legislation was judged to fall short of the standard set by the European Equal Pay Directive and had to be amended to conform to the European legislation.

The second positive development associated with the SAP and the 1970s concerned the raising of consciousness about equality issues and gender issues more generally. Part of this consciousness-raising had to do with broadly established feminist networks in domestic and transnational society. Part was also due to the work of extraordinary individuals, such as Éliane Vogel-Polsky of Belgium and Évélyne Sullerot of France. Vogel-Polsky was engaged in a decade-long struggle on behalf of Gabrielle Defrenne, in her legal actions against Sabena Airlines. Sullerot was an academic who wrote a book, *Histoire et Sociologie du Travail Féminin*, that was to catch the attention of Eurocrats (Hoskyns 1996, 83). As a result of this, she was asked by the Commission to prepare a report of a cross-national nature, rather than country by country, and this report was taken up by a Commission official in DG V, the Directorate for Social Affairs. While it is difficult to gauge the impact of individual activists, it is clear that the 1970s were a decade of some attention to women's causes. The United Nations identified 1975 as International Women's Year and held a massive conference in Mexico City to commemorate it. The EC sent a delegation, which raised the question of what the EC had to say about the matter of women's rights (Hoskyns 1996, 86). The Defrenne litigation (discussed below) and the pressure exerted by individual women and women's organizations significantly influenced important EC institutions, and in particular the Commission.

This is not to say that the 1970s were a decade of radical progress in social policy. The Equal Pay and Equal Treatment Directives did not have immediate and large-scale impact. Also, the seventies saw the descent into *Eurosclerosis*, a debilitating political-economic condition combining price inflation with slow growth. By 1979, the leading edge of a conservative front had pushed into Great Britain with Thatcher's electoral success, cooling any prospect of large-scale social progress (see Bashevkin 1996). By 1983, conservative and center-right governments had taken power in several European countries, intent on cutting back government expenditure and increasing the role of the market. This was not a fertile environment for capitalizing on the seeds sown by the Commission with its equality directives. As one commentator put it, "the Community's performance paled in comparison with the promise of the Paris Summit and the first Social Action Program" (Dinan 1994, 396).

Despite modest progress in the 1970s in the form of an action program and some framework legislation, the Fontainebleau Summit of 1984 provided the setting for the next major social policy initiative. By this time, conservative and center-right coalitions had come to power in many European countries, including the United Kingdom, Germany, Belgium, the Netherlands, and Denmark. In France, a struggle between two wings of the Socialist Party resulted in "The Great Turnaround" of 1983, in which the French were forced (by international capital markets) to pursue neo-liberal (free market) policies. In political and ideological terms, the leaders of many European countries were a much more conservative lot than their counterparts during the 1970s. Yet, while the main achievement of these leaders was the institution of a neo-liberal program at the European level (through the "1992" program, discussed below) these same leaders also gave a push to social policy development.

The leaders at this Summit and at the 1985 Milan Summit cleared the way for implementation of the Commission's 1985 White Paper on completing the Internal Market and laid the groundwork for the Treaty revisions which were ultimately incorporated into the Single European Act (SEA). The SEA set out the legislative program for completing the internal market by 1993 (the "1992 Project"). This program consisted of 279 Directives, each one dealing with a specific aspect of a unified market. Social policy advanced very little with the SEA, with the exception of the extension of the cooperation procedure–which increased the European Parliament's influence—and Council qualified majority voting to the area of worker health and safety under Article 118 (see Vogel-Polsky 1989 and Banks 1993 for assessments).

While hopes for expansive social policy provisions in the SEA went unrealized, during 1989 the Commission drew up a Community Charter of the Fundamental Social Rights of Workers. In December 1989 eleven of twelve EC members (all but the United Kingdom) signed the Charter which, while containing many goals supported by at least some EC gov-

ernments, did not go very far. Indeed, Vogel-Polsky (1990, 219) character-
izes the December 1989 Strasbourg Summit at which the Charter was
adopted as a "searing defeat" for Community social policy. The Charter is
a "solemn declaration" of good intentions and as such does not have immediate legal consequences. To be most effective, its provisions must be
implemented through specific legislation (see Box 2.2) (Hepple 1990).

Since the Charter was not legally binding, the EC seemed to be at an
impasse regarding social policy. To make matters worse, enacting most
social policy legislation would require unanimity among the member
states. Since the Single European Act, Article 100a (Article 95 post-
Amsterdam) has allowed for harmonizing measures necessary to establish the internal market to be adopted by qualified majority. However,
this provision excludes measures relating to the free movement of persons and "the rights and interests of employed persons." Meeting at
Maastricht in 1991 to negotiate what eventually became the 1993 Treaty
on European Union (TEU), member states could not reach unanimous
agreement on including more expansive measures in the core of the
treaty. Faced with this impasse, EU states designed a two-speed social
policy track. Eleven states (all EU members minus the United Kingdom)
signed a special protocol to the Treaty known as the Social Protocol, to
avail themselves of the procedures and resources of the Treaty in matters
of social policy. The Protocol did permit adoption of social policy measures by qualified majority. However, until the wholesale integration of
these articles into the body of the 1999 Treaty of Amsterdam, this arrangement remained unwieldy and constitutionally ambiguous.

The European Commission, led during this period by French socialist
Jacques Delors, proposed a wide range of social legislation. It proved especially adept at playing the "treaty base game," that is, at expansively
(and creatively) reading Treaty articles permitting majority voting in the
Council in an attempt to circumvent the unanimity rule (and, in most
cases, the British veto) (Rhodes 1995a). Despite meaningful progress in
areas governed by qualified minority voting (QMV) (especially worker
health and safety [Banks 1993]), overall results were modest. Judged in
light of the fate of these initiatives and the Council of Minister's meager
legislation in this area, social policy as a whole could not be judged a success. It is difficult to disagree with Leibfried and Pierson's conclusion that
the story (of social policy accomplishments) " has been a saga of high as-
pirations and modest results, marked by cheap talk proffered in the confi-
dent knowledge that the unanimity required for Council votes would
never be reached and that ambitious blueprints would remain unexe-
cuted" (Leibfried and Pierson 1995, 46).

Member states took steps forward at Amsterdam by incorporating the
Social Protocol into the body of the Treaty and extended qualified major-

Box 2.2　Legislative Instruments in the EU

Broad statements of political principles require implementation through binding legislation, which in the EU can take any of several forms. According to Article 249 of the Amsterdam Treaty (ex-Article 189), the Commission, Council, and Parliament (acting jointly with the Council) can "make regulations and issue directives, take decisions, make recommendations or deliver opinions." Of these, regulations are the strongest EU legal instrument. They are binding and directly applicable in all member states. Once published in the EU *Official Journal* (OJ), they become national law without further action by the member states. Directives, such as the 279 acts foreseen in the 1985 White Paper that formed the core of the "1992" single market program, are the next strongest instruments. They address themselves to member states and are specific as to their goals but not as to the means of achieving those goals. Member states must thus implement directives by passing national legislation. Decisions have binding force but remain quite weak. Opinions and recommendations are the weakest official instruments, constituting statements of position or principle that lack binding force. In contrast to these treaty-sanctioned instruments, resolutions, declarations, and other acts (such as the 1989 Social Charter) are legally ambiguous and lack binding force.

ity voting to selected areas, including the equal pay provisions of article 141 (ex Article 119). Indeed, Duff suggests laconically that "if one of the main objectives of Amsterdam was to resolve some of the worst problems of [the 1993 Maastricht Treaty], nowhere was it more successful than in the field of social policy" (Duff 1997, 72). Despite this modest progress, Treaty provisions remain thin and still frequently employ unanimity procedures, Council legislation remains relatively meager, and the prospects for immediate improvement remain slight.

The impression of a weak social policy for Europe is reflected in the budgetary figures. The total EU budget is quite small, just over 1 percent of the collective gross domestic product of the member states. This same budget is about 3 to 4 percent of total "domestic" public expenditures. Since the "social budget" at the EU level is small, the ratio of EU social spending to combined welfare spending at the national level is 0.9 percent (Gomà 1996,

222). Whether this fiscal constraint is treated as a cause or symptom, it nevertheless underlines a weak European-level social policy.

In the following section, I take a second look at EU social policy. This time I focus less on the Commission and Council of Ministers, less on the grand bargains among heads of state, and more on the piecemeal efforts of the ECJ and private litigants to fashion a social policy relying on admittedly weak Treaty provisions. This reaction leads to a surprisingly different conclusion.

THE EVIDENCE: ANOTHER LOOK

In the last section, I established that the grand initiatives of the European Commission came to relatively little when judged by the standard of adoption by the Council of Ministers. As a result, the legislative basis for social policy in the EU remains quite weak. EU citizens do not have a strong statutory basis for claiming social policy rights. However, the legislative route is not the only way to achieve social policy. Given the territorially fragmented nature of the EU political system, the existence of power centers at different levels, centrally directed change is difficult. The center is weak. There is no strong executive that is elected by the people, and the Council of Ministers takes decisions on most important questions by unanimity. In the area of social policy, the unanimity rule means that nothing gets done unless all fifteen memberstates agree. Thus it is easier to obstruct than to pass important initiatives at any point in time.

In order to move ahead, some way had to be found around this impasse. For various reasons, it was the European Court of Justice (ECJ) that led the way. The Court, despite its cumbersome structure (one judge from each member state), operates by a simplified set of rules. Court judgements are made on the basis of a simple majority, proceedings are held in secret, and no dissenting opinions are published. Thus, if the Court can "find" justification for something in the Treaty, it effectively reverses the institutional dynamics of the Council of Ministers. Whereas the Council has to agree unanimously for a social policy provision to pass, the Court, if it interprets such provisions to be implied by the Treaty, automatically requires the unanimous consent of the Council to reverse it.

Having said this, it still remains true that, by all appearances, the framers of the Rome Treaty did not expect the ECJ to wield substantial power, least of all in the area of social policy. It is precisely in this area where established welfare states control the important redistributive programs, which are in turn tied to powerful electoral constituencies. Yet, on the basis of limited treaty provisions, the ECJ has accounted for a significant jurisprudence in some areas of social policy.

CONSTITUTIONALIZATION OF THE ROME TREATY

The landmark judgments in social policy were set forth during the 1970s, 1980s, and 1990s. One essential characteristic of these cases involved the conferring of rights and responsibilities on individuals. It is difficult to exaggerate the importance of this process because it was precisely this condition which did not exist at the time the Rome Treaty was signed. To see this, we have just to remind ourselves that the Rome Treaty was just that, an international treaty, a compact among sovereign states. A treaty, or international compact, implies two things. First, it implies that states are the signatories and parties to the agreement. As such, states create and take up obligations and exercise rights. Individuals and other actors such as corporations do not have legal standing, and no legal standing implies no judicial remedy.

Second, an international treaty leaves the relation between domestic (municipal) law and international law unsettled. Three different relationships are possible. A state may declare that, when a conflict exists, international law rules; it may say the opposite, that domestic law rules; or it may devise another rule to deal with a possible conflict, such as *lex posteriori*, which means that the most recently enacted law, from whichever level of authority it emanates, holds sway. In the last case, if a conflict arises between, say, a British Parliamentary law and provisions of the Rome Treaty, and if the Parliamentary law appears later, then it is supreme. This is the essence of the *lex posteriori* doctrine.

Without legal standing for individuals and in the absence of a clear doctrine about what to do in the event of a conflict between European law and domestic law, European social policy bearing on individuals was not conceivable. Yet we have elements of European social policy today, limited as it may be. How did this happen? How did the EU transform itself from an interstate treaty into something approaching a constitutional document akin to constitutions governing domestic society?

The name given to this transformation is *constitutionalization*. Constitutionalization refers to the process by which the European treaties were transformed from interstate compacts "into a vertically integrated legal regime conferring judicially enforceable rights and obligations on all legal persons and entities, public and private within EC territory" (Stone Sweet and Caporaso, 1998, 102). The Treaty, a classic instrument of intergovernmental relations, was constitutionalized by a series of bold judicial decisions that created judicially enforceable rights and responsibilities for individuals.

Two of the most important pieces of the constitutional architecture of the EU were put in place by the *Van Gend En Loos* and *Costa v. ENEL* cases. In the 1963 *Van Gend* case (Case 26/62, [1963] ECR 1), the Court established the principle of direct effect. This principle holds that certain provisions of EU law, particularly Treaty law and Regulations, confer on individuals legal rights that public authorities must respect. In the absence of such respect, individuals (private persons, corporations) may bring complaints before the ECJ and seek judicial redress. The *Van Gend* case is of historic significance. It effectively opens up a space in the international system for individuals to press their rights against public authorities in their own or other countries. Individuals are given a legal status that they previously enjoyed only within domestic society. Eleven years later, in the 1974 *Van Duyn v. Home Office* case (Case 41/74, [1974] ECR 1337), the Court extended the logic of direct effect to Directives. As noted in Box 2.2, Directives are a class of secondary legislation that is intended to be binding on states as to the result to be achieved but not as to the means to achieve it. This case engendered even more opposition to the Court, since Directives set up obligations to which states must comply, even if they have some flexibility as to how to fulfill these obligations. (Mancini 1991, 182). Notwithstanding this opposition, the judgment effectively extended the range of rights that individuals could claim.

The doctrine of direct effect may be viewed as necessary but not sufficient to provide judicial remedies to private persons. One piece of the constitutional architecture was still missing and this had to do with the relationship between European law and the laws of the domestic states that make up the EC. What happens when there is a conflict between European law and domestic law? Provisions for such conflicts are standard equipment in federal systems, that is, systems in which there is a territorial distribution of power, such as the United States, Canada, Australia, or Germany. Article 6 of the Constitution of the United States sets forth that "the laws of the United States. . . shall be the supreme law of the land; and judges in every state shall be bound thereby; anything in the constitution or laws of any state to the contrary notwithstanding." Similarly, the German basic law (the *Grundgesetz*) stipulates that federal law outweighs state [*Land*] law (Mancini 1991, 180). However, unlike the United States and the Federal Republic of Germany, there are no explicit provisions in the Rome Treaty for reconciling conflicts among multiple levels of government. Yet, without such a working principle, the doctrine of direct effect by itself would be of little help.

In 1964, just one year after the doctrine of direct effect had been advanced, a case came before the ECJ that offered it an opportunity to weigh in on the question of a conflict of laws. An Italian national, Mr. Costa, had been prosecuted by Italian authorities for failing to pay his (three dollar!) electricity bill. He argued that his rights had been infringed, since the Italian law nationalizing the electricity company was in violation of the Rome Treaty. Mr. Costa had already been turned down by the Italian Constitutional Courts. For Italy, the relation between domestic law and international law is governed by *lex posteriori*. Since the Italian (parliamentary) law was subsequent to the Rome Treaty, the former should apply. However, in its judgment (*Costa v. ENEL*, Case 6/64, [1964] ECR 585) the ECJ turned this line of reasoning down and argued that the member states had limited their own sovereignty by transferring powers from the States to the Community, thus binding themselves and their own nationals.

The Court's decisions regarding direct effect and supremacy might be seen as creating a deep conflict between national governments and European institutions, and indeed such conflicts were present. The United Kingdom, in particular, resisted the spread of European law at many turns. Even the French *Conseil d'État* and the German *Bundesfinanzhof* put up resistance. However, the process of constitutionalization also had strong roots in domestic society. In fact, this process was driven by the relationship between private litigants, national judges, and the European Court in the context of the Article 177 (post-Amsterdam Article 234) procedure, also known as the preliminary ruling procedure (for an in-depth examination see Slaughter, Stone Sweet, and Weiler 1998). Article 177 allows national courts, when they are considering cases in which European law is relevant, to ask for a preliminary reference (an advisory opinion of sorts) from the ECJ. Cases can then be referred to the ECJ which would then render an opinion. Domestic courts then pronounce on the cases before them with the advice of the ECJ. In this way, European law can become domestic law without cases being formally tried before any European court. This substantially lessens the antagonism between national and European levels.

THE COURTS AND SOCIAL POLICY

In this section, I will consider three areas of social policy: equal pay and equal treatment, pregnancy, and social security. Each of these areas builds on the Court's jurisprudence described above.

Equal Pay and Equal Treatment

The equal pay jurisprudence is based on Article 119 of the Rome Treaty that, as stated earlier, was included at France's insistence as a way of avoiding "social dumping."[1] In 1958 virtually no one thought that Article 119 would become a keystone in the Court's activist agenda. Imagining this would not have been easy, given that the "direct effect" and "supremacy" principles had not yet been established. Yet, on the basis of this flimsy Treaty provision, the ECJ established its social policy in the area of equal pay.

A landmark case in the field of equal pay is *Defrenne v. Sabena II* (Case 43/75, [1976] ECR 455). This is a case of forced job change. Having reached the age of 40, Ms. Defrenne, a Belgian national and airline stewardess for Sabena Airlines, was asked (that is, told) to take another job with Sabena or be "let go" (fired). After working through the national judicial system unsuccessfully, Ms. Defrenne brought her case to the European Court of Justice. The ECJ ruled in Defrenne's favor, pointing out that a male steward in the same position was not required to switch jobs. The Court went beyond the particulars of the case to state that "the fact that certain provisions of the treaty are formally addressed to member states does not prevent rights from being conferred at the same time on any individual who has an interest in the performance of the duties thus laid down" (Case 43/75, *Defrenne v. Sabena*, [1976] ECR 455, point 31). It went on to say that Article 119 imposed a duty on states to ensure application of the equal pay principle and that, given the precise nature of that obligation, domestic courts could use the provision to enforce individual rights.

The *Defrenne* case provided an important victory for the Court, and it did not come without opposition. The United Kingdom, in particular, was opposed and pursued a clear strategy in the Council of Ministers, one designed to anticipate and then seal off pathways that might lead to the erosion of national by supranational authority. It systematically refused to support secondary legislation on the subject of equal pay for equal work and it consistently wrote detailed exceptions to the proposed rules in order to accommodate British national laws (Stone Sweet and Caporaso 1998, 123). Despite this opposition, the ECJ succeeded in setting down a Court-led social policy in the area of equal pay.

The *Defrenne* case was the start of a long line of equal pay cases. In these cases, the Court interpreted the Treaty, as well as Directives, expansively, despite the opposition of some member states. In doing so, it extended the logic of equal pay to areas that might not have been included under the original meaning of the term. The Court's jurisprudence took two routes. First, the ECJ expanded the meaning of "pay." Second, the Court gradually broadened the idea of discrimination to include indirect as well as direct forms of it.

Article 119 of the Rome Treaty on "equal pay" only provided the broadest guidance as to what equal pay meant in practice. In particular, there was no guidance as to whether the equality provisions applied only to wage income or to other categories of remuneration, such as pensions, fringe benefits, company cars and so forth. Also, it was not clear if the "equality" part of the equal pay provisions applied only to work for identical jobs or jobs that were comparable in the value they created. The Court took a relatively narrow line up to the mid-seventies when it started to interpret cases more expansively. The "equal value" provision of the Equal Pay Directive (1975) provided a lever with which the Court could argue that the idea of equality applied not only to pay for identical work but also for work of equal value. Among the benefits now included under the equal pay provisions are statutory sick pay, payments under private occupational pension schemes, redundancy payments, rules that govern automatic passage to a higher salary grade, and paid leave or overtime pay for staff members participating in events or courses to further their skills (Cox 1993, 43).

The next big challenge for the ECJ lay in extending the concept of discrimination from direct to indirect forms. Direct discrimination is relatively simple and straightforward. If a man and a woman are performing the same job, say that of a cutter in a garment factory, and they are paid different wages, this is direct discrimination. However, suppose that a company has a policy of restricting its holiday or vacation benefits to full-time workers. Part-time workers do not receive the same benefits or the proportionate benefits suggested by the number of hours worked. If women are disproportionately represented among part-time workers, the policy of this company might be judged discriminatory in result if not in intent. In other words, indirect discrimination applies to situations where individuals are not necessarily acting with discriminatory intent, but where their actions have discriminatory consequences. Article 1 of the Equal Pay Directive (1975) calls not only for equal pay for equal work or work to which equal value is attributed, but also "for the elimination of all discrimination on grounds of sex with regard to all aspects and conditions of remuneration" (Ostner and Lewis 1995, 169). This is broad language that suggests that discrimination should not be interpreted in narrow terms.

The ECJ responded to the Equality Directive, as well as Article 119, by bringing indirect discrimination under the provisions of equal pay and equal treatment. In the *Bilka* case, a German department store excluded part-time workers from its occupational pension scheme. From a strictly economic standpoint, it is easy to imagine why this might be attractive from the employer's point of view. A dual labor market is created—full-time workers and part-time workers—that can be manipulated by the employer, for example, by intensifying work in the part-time sector and slowing it down in the full-time sector. Or one can use the part-time sector as an implicit threat to the wage demands of the full-time sector and so on. Many options are available in this "flexible" labor market. The ECJ, however, took a moderate line and struck down the department store's right to deprive part-time workers of pension benefits, but only because they had not demonstrated a real (meaning material) justification. Nevertheless, the Court ruled that all elements of pay are due to workers, regardless of the number of hours worked (Ostner and Lewis 1995, 170).

Pregnancy

The second area of the Court's jurisprudence examined here concerns pregnancy and work. This area also illustrates the potential of the "equal treatment" provisions of EU law. What does European social policy have to say about the hiring and firing of pregnant women, maternity leave, reemployment, and day care centers? Until very recently, the answer has been "not much." However, this is changing too as the Court develops a jurisprudence in the area of pregnancy and work.

One of the first landmark cases was *Dekker v. Vormingcentrum* (Case C-177/88, [1990] ECR I-3941). A woman who had been denied a teaching position at a youth training center brought the case before a Dutch court, which then referred it to the ECJ. When she applied for the position, Ms. Dekker was three months pregnant and she so informed the Center's hiring committee. The Center's hiring committee informed Ms. Dekker that she was the most qualified candidate for the job. In spite of this, they could not hire her because their employment insurance did not cover sick leave for illnesses that (a) would occur during the first six months of employment if (b) these illnesses could be foreseen at the time of hiring.

The lower courts in the Netherlands found against Dekker. When the matter came before the Dutch Supreme Court, the Court asked the ECJ for an interpretation of the national law (governing reimbursements for pregnancy) based on the 177 procedure. At issue was Article 2 of the Equal Treatment Directive prohibiting employment discrimination on the grounds of sex, marital status, or family status. Dekker, supported by the European Commission, argued that the Center's decision constituted sex discrimination, since only women and not men can become pregnant. They also argued that pregnancy was not "illness," *une maladie prévisible*. The ECJ found in favor of Dekker, ruling that the Center's refusal to hire her clearly violated Article 119 and the Equal Treatment Directives. The source of the problem lay in the fact that the Dutch national legislation equated pregnancy with sickness and did not see it as *sui generis*, and therefore as an exception to the rule that allowed the insurance agency to refuse to pay.

A second case, *Webb* (Case C-32/93, [1994] ECR I-3567), concerned a woman who was hired by an air cargo company to replace a female clerk on maternity leave. During her training period, Ms. Webb found that she too was pregnant. The company dismissed her. Webb lost a succession of appeals, including a unanimous judgement by the highest British Court. The case was referred to the ECJ, which again found in favor of Webb. In doing so, the ECJ effectively overruled the law of the land as decided by the highest British Court. These two cases opened up a floodgate of claims from women who had been discharged from the British Armed Services on the grounds that pregnancy made them unable to perform their duties. After the ECJ's decisions in this area, national authorities had to settle with claimants at great financial cost.

Social Security

The third area of social policy considered here concerns the harmonization of social security across borders.[2] Social security, broadly conceived, refers to governmental income for old age and retirement, usually based on contributions from earned income. The need for such harmonization arises out of numerous and quite conflicting practical problems associated with the movement of workers in the European market. Questions arise about residence requirements and place of work insofar as benefits are concerned, the nature of these benefits, who should decide on them, who is entitled to receive them, and where they are to be consumed.

The starting point for understanding the transnational aspects of social security lies with national governments since nation-states have been the vehicles for developing social security schemes. Social security policies have typically been jealously guarded by national elites. In addition, the member states of the EU have different conceptions regarding the content of social policy. Even if the members treated EU migrants exactly the same as their own nationals, they would still be applying different policies, so long as fifteen different national systems of social security were in place. National authorities continue to use territorial principles to organize the content of their social policies. As Rob Cornelissen put it, national authorities "confine their social security schemes to people who work in their territory (the Bismarckian model) or who reside in their territory (the Beveridge and Nordic models); they guarantee benefits to those who have worked or resided for a certain period of time under the social security scheme of their country; they guarantee family benefits to insured people whose children reside on the territory of their country, and they guarantee the payment of certain benefits to those who reside in the territory of their country; etc." (Cornelissen 1996, 440–441).

Yet, ever since the Rome Treaty, Article 48 (post-Amsterdam Article 39) has established that workers in any member state have the right to move to another member state to work there, and to settle in another country with their families. Furthermore, secondary legislation (Regulation 1408/71) lays down that persons residing in the territory of one member state where certain provisions apply to nationals are subject to the same obligations and enjoy the same benefits under its legislation as nationals of that state (Cornelissen 1996, 440). This principle, free movement of workers, stands in contrast to the national control of social security policy.

It is important to recognize that the Treaty provisions about non-discrimination in no way logically impede national authorities from using territorial control and traditional conceptions of sovereignty to alter the content of their own social policy. Thus, the main question is "what happens when workers can move freely across borders but when national states have the capacity to make laws so as to preserve key elements of territorial sovereignty?" How might territoriality, particularly in its strongest form of exclusive sovereign rule, be preserved, eroded, or simply altered? I will examine three distinct areas of social security policy to try to gain purchase on this question.

Aggregation of Benefits.   What happens when a worker completes part of his or her life's work in one country and another part in a different country? It is quite possible that the minimum number of years required to collect benefits (or full benefits) will not be met in either country. A worker who works 14 years in Italy and four years in Germany satisfies the minimum conditions neither for an Italian pension (15 to 20 years) nor a German pension (minimum of five years) (Cornelissen 1996, 451). Here the market and territoriality are disconnected in such a way as to prevent benefits from being collected. The Court has already made decisions in this area so as to harmonize international complications arising from workers moving across national lines.

The limitations on free movement of workers stemming from lack of harmonized laws on requirements of benefits are responded to in two ways. First, the Council of Ministers has passed legislation designed to shore up the gaps in domestic law. Regulation 1408 in 1971 attempts to provide for coordination with regard to sickness and maternity insurance, old-age and survivors' pensions, invalidity, unemployment benefits, and family benefits. (Cornelissen 1996, 451) Second, the ECJ has interpreted the Treaty as providing a broad basis for non-discrimination, using the free movement provisions of the Treaty of Rome. If welfare benefits could be denied for reasons having to do, directly or indirectly, with movement of workers from one country to another, it would amount to discriminatory treatment. The Court has just begun to tackle cases of this type, but there is one recent case that bears on the matter. This case arose out of the denial by Dutch authorities of cash benefits to a Dutch woman, Ms. Klaus, who had worked successively in the Netherlands, Spain, the Netherlands, and Spain once again. She was denied benefits because of a provision of Dutch law stating that no cash benefits should go to a person who, at the moment of entry into the insurance scheme, was not capable of work. After being turned down by the Dutch social security institution, she appealed her case to a Dutch Tribunal who put questions to the ECJ under the Article 177 procedure. The Court rendered a judgement that supported Ms. Klaus, saying that "the working life of the person concerned should be seen *as a whole,* and not just from the limited standpoint of a particular job in one country, at one period of time" (Cornelissen 1996, 453).

Residence and Pensions.   Some states require residence in the country of employment in order for pensions to be paid. This would mean that a Danish worker who had worked his or her entire life in Denmark could not choose to retire in Portugal and collect benefits. Or, even more striking, it would mean that an Italian worker who had worked in Germany could not retire in Italy (his or her country of origin) and collect benefits. Such territorially-based provisions are obviously prejudicial to migrant workers. Having taken advantage of the region-wide market, and having accumulated a pension, the worker must choose between the benefits and preferred place of living. Legislation passed by the Council of Ministers (Article 10 of Regulation 1408/71) has waived residence requirements and the ECJ has aggressively interpreted Council Regulations so as to broaden the scope of their application. The Court has decided, again using the free movement provisions of the treaty as well as secondary legislation, that a pension already acquired cannot be subject to a residence condition and also that one cannot be denied entitlement to a pension solely because of residence in another member state (Cornelissen 1996, 455).

Territoriality and Unemployment Benefits.   What happens when a person employed in a foreign member state becomes unemployed? Whose laws apply? How long does the worker have to work in a different member state before he or she becomes eligible for benefits? Do these benefits apply fully? Suppose the worker has a spouse and dependents? Do the full allowances apply, including increased support for spouse and dependents, and if they do apply, does this coverage extend to the circumstance in which dependents live in the home country (not the country where the worker is employed)? These are tricky questions for which no full-blown answer is provided, either by the Court, the treaties, or by secondary legislation. Many countries have provision for increased benefits for workers with dependents, including migrant workers with dependents, as long as they reside in the state in question. Dutch legislation, for example, ties such increases for dependents to the requirement that these dependents actually live in the Netherlands.

The Court has begun to test these national legislative requirements, and although it is still too early to know what the outcome will be, there are some indications. In some ways, the Court has interpreted rights to unemployment benefits restrictively, for example, an unemployed person can claim the right to unemployment benefits only under the legislation of the state in which he or she became unemployed (Cornelissen 1996, 457). However, the free movement provisions of the Treaty are quite powerful. Since these provisions are recognized in a comprehensive way for the movement of goods, services, and productive factors, it is not surprising that the Court takes a broad view of them as applied to the movement of workers. This is most clearly illustrated in the *Acciardi* case (Case C-66/92, [1993] ECR I-4567). Mr. Acciardi was an Italian national who worked in the Netherlands and received Dutch unemployment benefits and special benefits for persons with partial incapacity to work. A provision of the Dutch legislation stated that the amount of the benefits was to be increased for dependents, so long as the members of the family of the unemployed worker resided in the Netherlands. Mr. Acciardi's wife and child resided in Italy. The ECJ ruled that residence was irrelevant to the reception of benefits and ordered the Dutch agency to pay the additional allowances (Cornelissen 1996, 458).

CONCLUSION

At the beginning of this chapter I identified two dilemmas of European integration in the area of social policy. The first dilemma pointed to the relationship between national social policy and European regional social policy. Is integration at the European level bypassing or replacing established domestic social policies? The second dilemma raised the issue of the nature, scope, and significance of social policy. Since I found that elements of a European social policy do exist, I then went on to ask about its importance. The main focus of the second dilemma has to do with two different conceptions of citizenship, one flowing from membership in a political system, or state, and the other stemming from participation in the market.

Many argue that European social policy is weak at best and, to the extent that it exists at all, is controlled by domestic welfare states. These states cannot solve all their problems internally. People, in addition to goods and capital, cross borders, and when they do, complications arise. I identified a broad range of these complications, including recognition of credentials in job searches, equal pay for equal work, unemployment insurance, pensions, and maternity rights. To those who argue that social policy is weak, these examples only serve to prove the point that a limited transnational regime for social policy exists. Others point out that these social policy developments are not so insignificant and that they represent the outer edge of a new body of social policy law, backed by a European Court which has established supremacy with regard to domestic laws.

Whether the glass is half-empty or half-full is open to debate. But progress in social policy at the European level cannot be denied. The European Court of Justice has played a major role in moving ahead the social policy agenda, even while Jacques Delors (President of the Commission) was having little success with his Commission initiatives. The ECJ has constitutionalized important domains of activity by conferring on individuals certain rights and responsibilities. The Treaty as well as certain directives of the Council of Ministers are given direct effect, in turn implying that individuals have legal standing and can claim redress in the Court in light of European law. The ECJ has done this by relying on national courts rather than overriding them, a practice that has preempted opposition and increased the legitimacy of the Court of Justice.

The second dilemma concerns the underpinnings of European social policy. What are the foundations of social policy at the European level? How are such policies generated, how are they argued, and how are they justified?

Review of the process by which European social policy is constructed suggests that the evolution of social policy is strongly tied to the expansion of the European market. The main rights and responsibilities that are recognized in social policy relate to jobs, credentials (having them accepted across borders), occupational training, pay, unemployment insurance, pensions, and maternity rights related to work. A strong component of European social policy centers on gender equality but only in relation to women's role in the market. As Ostner and Lewis argue,

> EU policy toward women seems to have reached the limits of what may be expected in the current framework, and any new proposals are likely to be merely the unexpected or unintended byproducts of the increasingly complex politics of logrolling. The existing body of directives and rulings is sufficient to generate a continuing stream of important policy adaptations, but the two needles' eyes—the employment nexus and the constraints of member state cultural and political diversity—greatly narrow the space for EU policymaking (Ostner and Lewis 1995, 193).

NOTES

1. Social dumping occurs when firms from one country capitalize on the cost advantage generated by stricter regulations in another country—that is, tougher pollution laws or more costly social regulation—to sell their own goods there.

2. In this section I rely heavily on Cornelissen (1996) and Caporaso and Jupille (1997).

REFERENCES

Balassa, Bela. 1961. "Towards a Theory of Economic Integration." *Kyklos* 14 1:1–14.
Banks, Karen. 1993. "L'article 118a: élément dynamiqe de la politique sociale communautaire." *Cahiers de Droit Européen* 29, nos. 5–6:537–554.

Bashevkin, Sylvia. 1996. "Tough Times in Review: The British Women's Movement During the Thatcher Years." *Comparative Political Studies* 28, no. 4 (January):525–552.

Caporaso, James A., and Joseph Jupille. 1997. "Sovereignty, Citizenship, and the Europeanization of Social Policy," presented at the second workshop on Europeanization and Domestic Structural Change, University of Pittsburgh, Pittsburgh, Pa., November 7–8.

Caporaso, James A., and David P. Levine. 1992. *Theories of Political Economy*. New York: Cambridge University Press.

Cornelissen, Rob. 1996. "The Principle of Territoriality and the Community Regulations on Social Security (regulations 1408/71 and 574/72)." *Common Market Law Review* 33:439–471.

Cox, Susan. 1993. "Equal Opportunities." In *The Social Dimension: Employment Policy in the European Community*, edited by Michael Gold. New York: Macmillan.

Dinan, Desmond. 1994. *An Ever Closer Union?* Boulder, Colo.: Lynne Rienner Publishers.

Duff, Andrew, ed. 1997. *The Treaty of Amsterdam: Text and Commentary*. London: Sweet & Maxwell.

Dutheillet de Lamothe, Olivier. 1993. "Du traité de Rome au traité de Maastricht: la longue marche de l'Europe sociale." *Droit Social* no. 2 (February):194–200.

Gomà, Richard. 1996. "The Social Dimension of the European Union: A New Type of Welfare System." *Journal of European Public Policy* 3, no. 2 (June):209–230.

Harding, Christopher, and Ann Sherlock. 1995. *European Community Law: Text and Materials*. London and New York: Longman.

Hepple, Bob. 1990. "The Implementation of the Community Charter of Fundamental Social Rights." *Modern Law Review* 53, no. 5 (September):643–654.

Hoskyns, Catherine. 1996. *Integrating Gender: Women, Law, and Politics in the European Union*. London and New York: Verso Publications.

Krasner, Stephen D. 1999. *Sovereignty: Organized Hypocrisy*. Princeton, N.J.: Princeton University Press.

Leibfried, Stephan, and Paul Pierson. 1995. "Semisovereign Welfare States: Social Policy in a Multitiered Europe." In *European Social Policy: Between Fragmentation and Integration*, edited by Stephan Leibfried and Paul Pierson. Washington, D.C.: The Brookings Institution.

Mancini, G. Federico. 1991. "The Making of a Constitution for Europe." In *The New European Community: Decisionmaking and Institutional Change*, edited by Robert O. Keohane and Stanley Hoffmann. Boulder, Colo.: Westview Press.

Marks, Gary. 1992. "Structural Policy and Multilevel Governance in the EC." In *The State of the European Community*, vol. 2, edited by Alan W. Cafruny and Glenda G. Rosenthal. Boulder, Colo.: Lynne Rienner Publishers.

Marshall, T. H. 1975. *Social Policy*. 4th ed. London: Hutchinson Press.

Ostner, Ilona, and Jane Lewis. 1995. "Gender and the Evolution of European Social Policies." In *European Social Policy: Between Fragmentation and Integration*, edited by Stephan Leibfried and Paul Pierson. Washington, D.C.: The Brookings Institution.

Rhodes, Martin. 1995a. "Subversive Liberalism: Market Integration, Globalization and the European Welfare State." *Journal of European Public Policy* 2, no. 3:384–406.

———. 1995b. "A Regulatory Conundrum: Industrial Relations and the Social Dimension." In *European Social Policy: Between Fragmentation and Integration*, edited by Stephan Leibfried and Paul Pierson. Washington, D.C.: The Brookings Institution.

Skocpol, Theda. 1995. *Social Policy in the United States*. Princeton, N.J.: Princeton University Press.

Slaughter, Anne-Marie, Alec Stone Sweet, and Joseph Weiler, eds. 1998. *The European Court and National Courts: Doctrine and Jurisprudence*. Oxford: Hart Publishing.

Stone Sweet, Alec, and James A. Caporaso. 1998. "From Free Trade to Supranational Polity: The European Court and Integration." In *Supranational Governance: The Institutionalization of the European Union*, edited by Wayne Sandholtz and Alec Stone Sweet. Oxford: Oxford University Press.

Streeck, Wolfgang. 1995a. "From Market Making to State Building: Reflections on the Political Economy of European Social Policy." In *European Social Policy: Between Fragmentation and Integration*, edited by Stephan Leibfried and Paul Pierson. Washington, D.C.: The Brookings Institution.

———. 1995b. "Neo-Voluntarism: A New European Social Policy Regime." *European Law Journal* 1:31–59.

Vogel-Polsky, Éliane. 1989. "L'Acte unique ouvre-t-il l'espace social européen?" *Droit Social* no. 2 (February):177–189.

———. 1990. "Quel futur pour l'Europe sociale après le sommet de Strasbourg?" *Droit Social* no. 2 (February):219–227.

THREE

□   □   □

Dilemmas of Democracy
in the European Union

THE MEANING OF DEMOCRACY

As the European Union creates it own rules and institutions, as it becomes more important in everyday policymaking, in short, as it becomes
more like a domestic polity than a traditional international organization,
the issue of democracy becomes more central. No one asked the members
of the balance of power system in Europe to conduct their collective business in a democratic way, whether or not they were domestically organized as democracies. Even slightly more organized forms of international association such as the Concert of Vienna or the League of Nations
or the United Nations only partly subscribed to democratic principles.
According to balance of power logic, leaders of countries were expected
to pursue their interests on the basis of their respective power capabili-
ties, and not to seek the votes of other members of the international system in order to do so. All of this seems quite obvious. Nation-states in the
international system follow rules that are quite different from the rules
that individuals follow within states. We can agree to these differences
without creating a stereotype of the international system as an unruly an-
archy and domestic society as a harmonious polity under the rule of law.
We have only to compare the EU to the nineteenth-century balance of
power system, or to a traditional international organization, to see that
this is true.

DEFINITIONS

The broadest definition of democracy is governmental rule associated
with the people. I say "associated with" to avoid the controversy about

whether democracy means rule "by," or "on behalf of," the people. Norberto Bobbio states that democracy, or a democratic regime, "is taken to mean first and foremost a set of procedural rules for arriving at collective decisions in a way which accommodates and facilitates the fullest possible participation of interested parties" (1987, 19). Democracy is therefore a set of procedures about how collective decisions are taken. Collective decisions are decisions that bind the collectivity, or the relevant people within it. To be democratic, according to this definition, implies that the people choose both those who make the decisions (their representatives) and the procedures by which these decisions are made.

However, beyond this general meaning that people must be involved in making their own decisions, democracy can mean many things. The term usually implies political competition, rather than a monopoly of power, at all levels of government. That is why the terms constitution and democracy are so closely related. Constitutionalism as a political philosophy implies limited government. As Carl J. Friedrich has shown in his *Constitutional Government and Democracy* (1937), the forms which these limitations may take are numerous: free press (checking the exercise of executive or legislative power), separation of powers among legislatures and executives, an independent judiciary, and federalism (a territorial division of powers). Democracy also usually signifies an active participant political culture, with a citizenry willing to assume the responsibility of self-rule. This in turn implies voting, lobbying, willingness to take the time to influence one's representatives and so on. An active associational life is stressed by nineteenth-century theorists such as Alexis de Tocqueville and modern scholars such as Robert Putnam (1993). However, democracy takes time. (George Bernard Shaw once said that the problem with socialist democracy is that it takes too many nights, meaning that democracy only works with much discussion.) Since most people place political activity lower than other pursuits, no society can sustain democracy everywhere. This is why social pluralists and contemporary social democrats such as Wolfgang Streeck (1997) ardently advocate workplace democracy. The list could be expanded: multiple political parties, orderly succession of governments, representative legislatures and so on.

RELATIONSHIP BETWEEN DEMOCRACY AND MARKETS

The central dilemma of this chapter involves the relationship between democracy and markets. To understand better this dilemma, let me first turn to the market and say a word about this institution. A market is generally thought of as a private institution involving voluntary exchange. Coercive exchanges such as "your wallet or your life" or "if you don't remove those missiles from your bases we will bomb you" are implicit exchanges, but we usually call them threats. Market exchanges, on the other hand, are supposed to make the parties to transactions better off. If I am to buy the goods you want to sell, I must be convinced that the money I part with is worth less to me than the goods I receive, just as you must be convinced that the money you receive is worth more to you than the goods with which you might part. When markets work well, they facilitate voluntary exchanges and ensure that costs and benefits are restricted to the involved parties. When these conditions are met, markets all but ensure mutual benefits.

Now what about the relationship between democracy and markets? There are at least two theoretical points of view about this relationship. The first is that democracy and markets are not only compatible but that there is a strong affinity between them. This is a viewpoint to which many people would subscribe but is most famously associated with Milton Friedman (1962). The second argues just as strongly that these two institutions are antagonistic. While recognizing that democracy and markets coexist historically, they do so with a considerable amount of tension. This view is also shared by many, but its most famous contemporary expositors are Samuel Bowles and Herbert Gintis in *Democracy and Capitalism* (1986).

A number of comments can be made on behalf of Friedman's position that democracy and markets go together. First, we can note empirically, that capitalist markets and democracy are strongly associated. It is true that there are some capitalist states that are not (or were not) democracies (Argentina, Brazil, Mexico, and South Korea during certain phases of their development), but there are almost none that are democratic that are not also capitalist. Notice that capitalism is defined here in terms of markets and private ownership of capital and not in terms of high tax rates and redistributive politics. As a result, countries such as Denmark, Sweden, and Finland, which have very high rates of taxation (see Figure 3.1) and which use government revenues to redistribute wealth to poorer sections of society, are still essentially capitalist. They are categorized this way because the essential pillars of capitalism—markets and private property—are relied on to create wealth, while government taxation and social programs are used to equalize incomes and standards of living among different parts of the population. To sum up this point, democracy and capitalism are historically related to one another. Exceptions to this association are rare and seem to be concentrated among states that are undergoing modernizing development.

A second line of thinking relates to the linkages between markets and the kinds of psychological competencies required of individuals functioning in democracies. As mentioned above, democracy requires a society of individuals who are willing to do their own political work, even if that

FIGURE 3.1   Taxes and Social Contributions (as % 1994 GDP)

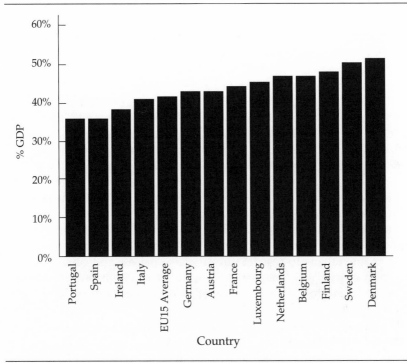

SOURCE: Eurostat, *Basic Statistics of the European Union*, 33rd edition
(Luxembourg: OOPEC, 1996), p. 53.

work only involves the selection of delegates who carry out the brunt of
the job. Thus, democracy suggests stronger forms of agency than other
kinds of government. It requires something called civic competence. The
argument here is that participation in markets prepares individuals for
democratic participation at the same time that democratic accountability
reinforces market behavior. Individuals in markets are continually called
upon to make their own decisions about how to acquire and dispose of
capital, if, when, and under what conditions to sell their own labor, which
technical mix to utilize in producing a particular product, at what level to
set prices in an industry (though if the industry is competitive there is not
much choice), and how to market the product in question.

A corollary to this argument is that markets are strongly related to self-
esteem, in both the positive and negative senses. Outcomes in markets are
more likely to be judged as "correct" results of individual merits and resources than outcomes in other settings. Robert Lane argues that "there is
a powerful causal connection between the emphasis on *exchange* in a mar-

ket economy and the belief among market participants that they are endowed with an internal locus of control" (Lane 1991, 157; emphasis in original). Since the market highlights human agency, it also creates a link between the costs and benefits flowing from the market and the flaws and merits of the participants. In the context of the market, benefits are "just rewards" and costs are "deserved penalties."

The third argument in favor of synergies between the market and democracy is that markets by definition imply economic decentralization, both of ownership of productive assets and allocative control. This decentralization is helpful if not critical in overcoming the tendency for political power to centralize. And, so the argument goes, dispersed private power is necessary to preserve organized political competition. Of course, in the real world, many corporations are huge, some of them generating income larger than the revenue of many nation-states. While the concentration of economic power is not unusual in capitalist democracies, it is seen as a "bad" thing, something to be fought with the appropriate antitrust policy. But the reason it is seen as bad is that concentrated economic power enables firms to restrict output, raise prices, and prevent other firms from entering the market. Although these reasons are important, they are different from the issue of whether or not concentrated economic power is bad for democracy.

In *Democracy and Capitalism* (1986), Samuel Bowles and Herbert Gintis pursue the opposite notion of conflict between democracy and market capitalism. To these two analysts, democracy means in part a domain of rights and obligations (freedom of speech, of association, freedom from unreasonable searches, right to vote, right to trial by jury) while market capitalism refers to commodities. The former domain, that of rights, implies universal distribution (every adult receives the same rights), the political guarantee that these rights will be enforced by the state, and bans on the exchange of these rights. People may not buy and sell votes (though candidates can spend money to attract voters), buy their way out of the obligation to serve in the armed services, and give up their right to a jury trial in return for money or a second vote. Rights legally prohibit the improvement of one's welfare through economic exchange and forbid the exploitation of comparative advantage within the political system. Mr. Smith, who fancies himself a sterling juror but may not stand the thought of being a soldier, cannot assume double duty as a juror and get out of his obligation to serve in the armed forces, even if Mr. Jones would love to complete such a trade with him. By setting up such prohibitions, our political institutions send out the message that there is something more important than economic exchange. There are some qualities so fundamental to being a person that one may not be deprived of them, even if one would like to do so at any particular moment.

What exactly should be in the domain of rights and what should be "merely" utilities that individuals are free to economize on, that is to trade? Most Americans would probably endorse as rights everything that is set forth as such in the Bill of Rights. Beyond this there would be more controversy. Should there be a right to a job, to a guaranteed income, to housing, to public education including a college education, and to medical care in old age? And what about private property rights? Beyond the general entitlement to hold property, what restrictions if any should apply to property ownership? Does private property include the right to exclude certain people from buying or selling? Does it include the right to burn trash on one's premises, to create pollution as a by-product of producing something else, or to create goods that may be dangerous to their users?

For Bowles and Gintis, the conflict between democracy and markets is clear. Liberal democracy endorses equality within the political system but not within the economic system. Every person has the same right to vote and the same right to trial by jury but does not have the same rights to income, job, and medical care. Depending on how one draws the line between the state and the market, the domain of rights may be small or large. If the market were purely private, as depicted above, the inequalities that exist would be less relevant. To be sure unequal resources still mean that some people will be better off than others, but this is only to recognize that in a liberal democracy there is a private and a public sector. Within this private space, individuals will differ depending on the resources with which they start (including inheritances), their respective efforts, their talent, and luck. Since these factors will vary greatly from individual to individual, inequalities will be large. But beyond this point, there is still the problem of the external consequences of "private" actions. The market is not a self-contained system where costs and benefits are perfectly channeled to those who bear responsibility. Markets regularly create external effects, what economists call externalities (see Box 3.1). The market thus becomes a system of unaccountable power. This is another way of saying that the market has social consequences that may need to be regulated. Recognition of these externalities does not justify elimination of the market, but it does point out clearly the dilemma between markets and democracy.

Let me see if I can sum things up. Bobbio has characterized the modern struggle of democracy as proceeding along two axes, one vertical and one horizontal (Bobbio 1987, 59, originally published 1984). The vertical dimension points to the struggle against the abuse of power by tyrants, dictators, and personal rulers who make policies that affect our lives. Democratic mobilization of the people, including the vote, involves an effort to check such abuses. The horizontal dimension points to the concentration of power in the hands of a few individuals, or of a single institution. A

Box 3.1 Externalities

When a market transaction affects someone not a party to it, it creates "*externalities.*" Some externalities are positive—for example, the benefit you derive from your neighbor's choice to landscape her yard. Of more direct political concern are negative externalities, which impose costs on non-parties to a transaction. For example, my decision to hire our common neighbor to incinerate my trash may force you to breathe polluted air. Whether one emphasizes the social injustices or the economic inefficiencies that externalities cause, most agree that externalities constitute market failures and justify recourse to political/governmental action, thus linking market activity and democratic control.

---

country where all powers are invested in the executive, even if he or she were popularly chosen, would indicate this type or concentration. Constitutional restrictions on the concentration of power and checks by some institutions of others are the remedy here.

Both dimensions of democracy are important because they relate to a higher principle, namely that for people to be free they must be self-governing, and to be self-governing, they must choose the leaders and the procedures which will bind them. When socially unaccountable power exists, as it can in the market, democratic forms of governance must be devised to bring these forces under popular control. Hopefully, this dilemma, between the market and democratic forms of governance, will set the stage for the next section on the European Union and the democratic deficit.

THE EUROPEAN UNION AND THE DEMOCRATIC DEFICIT

David Martin, a former vice president of the European Parliament, pointed to an interesting irony when he quipped that if the EC were a state and it applied for membership in the EC, it would be turned down because it is not sufficiently democratic (quoted in Dinan 1994, 288). This fanciful example serves to drive home an important point, namely, that the democratic credentials of the member states of the EU do not find a parallel in the democratic nature of the institution they have created. The "democratic deficit" alleged to exist at the European level is most acutely a deficit between the powers of national and EU executives and parliamentary institutions at both levels. This gap has become more pronounced as more and more powers are transferred to the European level where national ministers (appointed officials) decide and make laws without proportional legislative oversight. The gap is fundamentally about the relation between executive power and representative legislatures.

In the first several decades of the EU's development, few people worried about the non-democratic nature of its institutions. Indeed, the focus in the early phase was on survival and performance. How well would the EC fare in light of the challenges that would undoubtedly be placed before it? Would it succeed in resolving to the satisfaction of the six original member states the thorny problems of international trade, agricultural cooperation and restructuring, industrial transformation and so on? Looking back, we know the EU is a success. Its mandate has gone far beyond the original tasks it set for itself, it has added nine new members, and it has gone through a handful of treaty revisions. So growth, performance, and survival were the main goals. However, two powerful developments were to change all this and to generate a new set of expectations. These two developments had to do with the expansion of market relations across Europe and the growth of the EC's political institutions.

When the EEC came into existence in 1958, its main goals were the creation of a free trade area, a customs union, and a common agricultural policy (CAP). By 1968, it had made significant progress on all three fronts. Indeed, the free trade area and customs union were essentially in place by July 1, 1968, over a year ahead of schedule. After 1968 the Community seemed to languish (but see Golub 1999). It is true that the Court of Justice made important advances and that these advances were largely unrecognized by everyone except legal specialists. However, the main political arms of the Community failed to come up with a political agenda to match the importance of the goals of the first years.

However, while the Council of Ministers and the Commission were relatively quiet from 1968 to the early 1980s, two developments were taking place which were to affect the debate about the democratic character of the Community's institutions. The first had to do with the transformation of the transnational economy. The second concerned the development of Community institutions. While these activities were coupled, in the sense that the Single Market program simultaneously responded to transnational changes by expanding economic interactions regionally and provided the institutions for that expansion, they also developed in part on separate tracks.

Changes in the transnational economy occurred on a broad scale and involved the expansion and restructuring of trade, capital flows, market-

TABLE 3.1   Exports as Percentage of GDP, 1968–1997

	1968	1978	1988	1997
Belgium	39	46	59	68
Denmark	21	21	25	28
France	10	16	17	21
Germany	19	22	27	24
Ireland	27	44	54	73
Italy	13	19	15	21
Greece	6	11	8	7[a]
Spain	5	9	12	20
Portugal	14	14	23	23[a]
Netherlands	38	42	45	54
Luxembourg	70	64	74	41[a,b]
Austria	17	20	24	28[a]
Finland	19	25	21	33
Sweden	18	24	27	36
United Kingdom	16	21	17	22

SOURCE: International Monetary Fund, *International Financial Statistics Yearbook* (Washington, D.C.: IMF, 1998).
[a] Preliminary figures from International Monetary Fund, *International Financial Statistics* 52, 7 (July 1999).
[b] The precipitous drop in Luxembourg's 1997 figure represents rapid economic growth in the early 1990s unaccompanied by corresponding rises in exports. In particular, according to the IMF, Luxembourg experienced almost 33% GDP growth between 1990 and 1991 (*International Financial Statistics* 52, 7 [July 1999]: 583).

ing, and the behavior of firms. These changes involved an expansion of flows of goods, services, and productive factors across national borders. To some extent, this globalization process simply extended the processes by which nation-states took shape as economic units. The relative functionality of the nation-state, in comparison to city-states, small kingdoms, duchies, and feudal units was to be demonstrated over a period of several hundred years and was one of the most important aspects of the competitive survival of states in comparison to other units (Spruyt 1994). Local units of government simply could not compete with the nation-state in terms of protection of producers and traders, or in terms of enforcing contracts, providing justice, supplying money, and creating geographical environments of sufficient size as to allow for the most efficient divisions of labor and economies of scale.

By extension, the modern nation-state may be seen as too small, too constrained an economic environment for large, mobile modern firms. Luxembourg, Austria, Denmark, and Sweden are far below the optimum geographical size for economic efficiency. If they did not trade heavily,

TABLE 3.2   Intra-EU Exports as Percentage of all Exports, 1960–1996

	1960	1970	1975	1980	1985	1990	1996
Belgium/ Luxembourg	65.2	78.2	76.1	76.0	72.9	79.9	76.6
Denmark	68.6	64.9	64.8	67.4	59.7	68.4	67.5
Germany	52.7	59.3	56.1	60.5	58.6	64.0	57.1
Greece	48.4	56.7	54.4	49.6	56.7	68.0	52.0
Spain	64.7	52.0	50.8	54.1	55.3	67.6	66.8
France	41.9	60.8	55.9	58.1	56.5	65.3	62.1
Ireland	87.9	78.4	83.0	79.1	72.6	78.6	71.1
Italy	45.8	55.4	52.9	55.8	52.1	62.8	55.2
Netherlands	68.1	76.6	76.5	76.8	77.7	81.4	80.6
Austria	59.6	56.7	52.2	59.8	58.9	67.2	64.1
Portugal	42.1	52.5	63.6	65.7	68.7	81.2	80.0
Finland	62.0	64.0	56.3	57.7	51.0	62.2	54.5
Sweden	61.4	60.7	56.3	59.1	55.6	62.3	57.0
United Kingdom	28.6	40.0	41.7	50.0	54.0	57.3	57.8
EU 15 Average	49.4	59.7	58.0	61.0	59.9	66.8	62.9
Intra-EU Total (Bn ECU)	23.6	76.4	158.7	330.3	556.3	787.3	1058.4

NOTE: Table assumes constant (EU15) membership.
SOURCE: Eurostat, *External and Intra-European Union Trade: Statistical Yearbook, 1958–1996* (Luxembourg: OOPEC, 1997), p. 21.

and allow capital flows across their national borders, they would have a standard of living far below their current levels. Even if protection of producers and goods and services in transit is not as big a concern as it once was, the legal and cultural environments within which firms operate remain very important. Arrangements have to be made to allow incorporation of "foreign" firms, to facilitate the joining of host-country labor to capital from outside, to harmonize laws and product standards, and to stabilize expectations about the exchange rate environment.

Changes in the international trade environment involved an absolute expansion of imports and exports, an increase of both in relation to gross domestic product, and an increase in the ratio of trade within the region to total trade. These changes, taken together, tell us that trade has not only increased absolutely but in relation to the baselines of national production and trade with the rest of the world. Tables 3.1 and 3.2 provide data on trade as a fraction of gross domestic product (GDP) and on intra-EU trade in relation to total trade. Table 3.1 shows us clearly the progression of international trade from 1968 to 1997 by measuring total exports as a percentage of GDP. Bear in mind that the export figures represent total exports and not just those exports to other EU member states. In almost all cases, exports as a percentage of GDP rose from the time that the EC's customs union was established. Table 3.2 reports the exports within the EU region as a percentage of all exports. Here the figures are much higher since the comparison is with regard to total exports, rather than total domestic production. What is important here are the changes over time. In most cases, the share of exports within the region rises substantially over the period.

Intensified economic activity was not confined to regional trade. The activities of multinational corporations and banks were also important. The first wave of multinational activity in Europe was spurred by the surge of United States investment during the late fifties and early sixties. Ironically, it was U.S. firms that first responded to the coming into being of the EEC in 1958. U.S. firms were large, mobile, and on the outside. That is, they faced tariff and non-tariff barriers which European firms could soon expect to diminish. Thus, U.S. firms had an added incentive to jump over the external tariff walls set up by the customs union and invest directly in producing inside Europe.

A second wave of activity took place during the seventies. Part of the stimulus came from the relative stagnation of European economies during the seventies, a stagnation that was affected by the oil crisis and higher costs of energy inputs. But part of the movement took place as a result of a greater receptivity to business groups shown by the European Commission. During the late seventies, Etienne Davignon, EC Commissioner for Industry, worked closely with leaders of industry in their attempt to improve European competitiveness (Cowles 1997, 119). Davignon and business leaders, who later organized into the European Roundtable of Industrialists (ERT), considered proposals ranging from improvement of infrastructure (roads, communication) to restructuring of particular industries, to deregulation of the European market. Leaders of multinational firms figured prominently in Davignon's scheme of things and the ERT proved to be a powerful force that included membership among such firms as Bayer, Rhone-Poulenc, Olivetti, Nestle, and Volvo.

These firms lobbied intensively for changes in the economic, legal, and regulatory environments. These activities demonstrate clearly that multinational capital is not just an economic force that can be counted as so many dollars of foreign investment in host countries. On the contrary, multinational corporations are also a social and political force. These firms employ and lay off workers, make products and create externalities such as pollution, and lobby to change the laws and regulatory standards of a country in which they operate, not always in a more lax direction.

The overall point of this discussion of trade and multinational corporations is that the economic forces that they represent create pressure for political change. The biggest expression of this change was the passage in the mid-eighties of the Single European Act. This Act deepened the market in Europe by changing the regulatory environment, making it easier to conduct economic exchange across national borders. It also altered the institutional environment, to the consideration of which I now turn.

The second major development that cast the non-democratic nature of the EU into the spotlight had to do with institutions. To put it bluntly, as the institutions of the EU became more important, that is, as they grew and became responsible for more and more legislation and as more policy areas migrated from the national to the supranational level, people started to ask not only about the efficacy of these institutions but also about their representativeness and accountability. The original aims of the Community, while revolutionary by the standards of the time, seem modest today. The Rome Treaty set in place a political architecture that was to facilitate economic exchange and provide a framework for political cooperation in several other areas, chief of which was agriculture. The causal arrow foreseen by the founders of the Rome Treaty ran from political institutions to economic exchange. The possibility of strong feedback relations, through which economic exchange would create additional pressure for institutional change, was not anticipated. Yet, this is precisely what happened. Indeed, Stone Sweet and Sandholtz have organized an entire book around the EU's "remarkable transformation from an interstate bargain into a multi-dimensional quasi-federal polity" (1998, 1).

The most important original institutions of the Community represented a mix of territorial and non-territorial elements. That is, some institutions, such as the Council of Ministers, were set up directly to represent the interests of the member states. Each state, no matter how large or small, was to be represented by one minister, drawn from the relevant policy area (the minister of agriculture if farming was at issue, the minister of transport if transportation was at issue and so forth). On the other hand, the European Commission typified the more supranational aspect of Community institutions. While the individual Commissioners were appointed by the member state governments, they were not to receive instructions from their governments. Instead, the Commissioners were to draft legislation and set legislative priorities for the Council of Ministers. The European Parliament was to represent the populations of the countries but the members of Parliament were not directly elected (until 1979), and they furthermore did not have much by way of legislative power. Finally, the Court of Justice had one Justice from each member state appointed for a term of six years. The Court was to operate as an independent legal entity, much as we think of Courts acting in the United States, but in 1958 the powers of the Court were uncertain to say the least.

In sum, as Alberta Sbragia points out, the original institutions of the Community represented a complex mix of territorial and non-territorial elements (1993, 27–36). These institutions represent a "complex balancing act" (1993, 23) and remain the mainstay of the political structure of the EU today. However, they have changed a great deal. The Commission has to share its duties with a host of expert committees hardly recognized by the Rome Treaty. The EP is now directly elected and has gained legislative power through successive amendments to the original Treaty. The ECJ has established for itself the right to make rulings directly on individuals and to review legislation, both secondary legislation and domestic legislation, to see if it conforms to the basic law as set forth in the Treaties. In short, the Court has asserted (successfully) the right to judicial review and legal standing for individuals before Community law.

While the original structure of the Community was not particularly democratic, most people did not think this was a problem for two reasons. The first was that the Community was not seen as all that important. Its aims were rather limited, and beyond free trade and the common agricultural policy, it was not clear that this institution was going to fundamentally change the way politics were organized. Foreign and security policy, criminal justice, national planning, exchange rate, macroeconomic, and social policies all remained firmly in the hands of the individual states. Second, most of the decisionmaking in the early stages was taken through a laborious process of universal consent, that is, by seeking unanimity. Efforts to move beyond this to majority voting in 1965 provoked a constitutional crisis in which the French removed their representative in the Council of Ministers. The resolution of this crisis through the Luxembourg Compromise perpetuated the use of the veto (see Box 3.2).

As damaging as unanimity was in terms of holding back policymaking in many areas, it had one beneficial effect. It tended to deflect criticism from Community institutions for being non-democratic. So long as states could hold out to protect the interests of their own national constituency, citizens of these states could reason that they had some democratic mechanism at work in Brussels. Thus, when qualified majority voting (QMV) was extended to a great many new policy areas through the SEA in 1987, concern over democratic accountability heightened. This sets the stage for a discussion of the democratic deficit.

At the European level there is a disjunction between the transnational regional economy and the absence of a corresponding European state. Europe has a regional economy and a decentralized system of political authority. There is no inherent reason why politics, economics, society, and culture have to conform to the same scale requirements. Problems arise when the structure of political authority at the European level, particularly the balance of forces between executives and legislatures, differs from the corresponding balance of forces among domestic structures. To understand

Box 3.2   Luxembourg Compromise

In mid-1965, French President Charles de Gaulle initiated the "Empty Chair Crisis" by instructing French ministers to boycott all Council meetings. Finding its origins in a disagreement over the financing of the Community budget and the Common Agricultural Policy (CAP), the crisis came to revolve around majority voting in the Council and the relative power of member states and the supranational European Commission. After six months during which major Council business could not be conducted, EC member states struck the "Luxembourg Compromise" in January 1966. This "agreement to disagree" established that whenever a state invoked "vital national interests" on a topic at hand, discussion had to continue until unanimous consent was reached. It thus gave each state an effective veto over changes to the policy status quo. While a serious "constitutional crisis" in the short-term, these events had the longer term effect of stifling EC activity for almost twenty years (see, however, Golub 1999), creating a "Europessimism" to which the 1987 SEA was the perceived remedy. While some have hailed the death of the Luxembourg Compromise (Teasdale 1993), its use remains a possibility even in the contemporary EU (*Economist* 1995).

the nature of the democratic deficit we first have to understand the way that democratic forces are expressed in institutions domestically and compare these institutional structures to those at the European level.

Perhaps the clearest statement of the democratic deficit is given by Shirley Williams, a former member of Parliament in the United Kingdom:

The "democratic deficit" is the gap between the powers transferred to the Community level and the control of the elected Parliament over them, a gap filled by national civil servants operating as European experts or as members of regulation and management committees, and to some extent by organized lobbies, mainly representing business. One of the unforeseen consequences of the Community, therefore, beyond the transfer of sovereignty in specified areas, is the weakening of national parliaments vis-à-vis their own executives, even in those areas that lie outside Community competence at the present time (Williams 1991, 162).

In the member states of the EU, members of Parliaments are directly elected to represent the will of the people. They are to serve as a check on excessive executive power. Though admittedly the picture is idealized, representatives are to hold executive actions up to public scrutiny, to debate policy initiatives and pass on the results of such debates to the executives, and to serve as a focal point for public discussion about major policy initiatives. Since the power of the European Parliament is weak by comparison with national executives operating at the European level, executive power is correspondingly exercised without the "normal" checks that exist at the national level. As more and more authority migrates to the European level, as more and more policy is made in Brussels and not in national capitals, it follows that the deficit becomes wider. Executive power is enhanced, parliamentary power is diminished, and popular forces in general are excluded.

Furthermore, to the extent that lobbyists and national civil servants fill the void, this further aggravates the problem, in the sense that business interests are more likely to be represented by pressure groups. Those with the most mobile factors or production (capital rather than labor), and with the most concentrated interests (producers rather than consumers), are likely to gain disproportionately.

The democratic deficit is not about the loss of national power to supranational authorities *per se*. Rather it concerns the loss of legislative (representative) power to executives at both the national and supranational levels. National parliaments lose because authority to make decisions is no longer within their purview. The European Parliament does not pick up all of the corresponding national losses. Instead, this authority gravitates toward both national and supranational executives.

To understand how this works, let us take a look at the overall institutional structure of the EU. Primary executive power is vested in the Commission, which has the sole right of initiative but whose members are appointed by the member states. The original European Assembly (officially known since the Single European Act as the European Parliament [EP]) was composed of members chosen by national parliaments who were then sent to Brussels and Strasbourg. The powers of the EP were long considered quite limited, though the Single European Act, the Treaty on European Union (TEU), and the Amsterdam Treaty strengthened and extended these powers. In many areas (those covered by the codecision procedure, discussed below), the European Parliament acts as a co-legislator with the Council of Ministers. In other areas, legislative power rests firmly with the Council, a body that paradoxically is composed of national executives (Mancini and Keeling 1994, 175–176). The Commission is accountable to the Parliament in the sense that the Parliament can dismiss the Commission collectively, a power that it has now

Box 3.3   The Sacking of
the European Commission, 1999

The 1993 Maastricht Treaty gave the European Parliament the effective right to censure (that is, fire) the European Commission. While this right is commonly seen in parliamentary democracies, it represented a major innovation and an extension of democratic control in EU politics. Parliament first tried to exercise its newfound rights in early 1997, on the heels of the so-called "mad cow crisis," in which the Commission allegedly failed adequately to respond to threats to human health posed by tainted British beef. That effort failed. When allegations of fraud, nepotism, and internal mismanagement began surfacing against the European Commission in the late 1990s, the EP again rattled its saber. Under pressure, Commission president Jacques Santer agreed in January 1999 to the formation of a committee of independent experts that would investigate the allegations, and to abide by the committee's findings. Reporting in mid-March, the committee confirmed most of the allegations. With EP censure a near-certainty, Santer's Commission resigned *en masse* during the early morning hours on March 16th. The episode drove member state leaders to elect "one of their own," former Italian prime minister Romano Prodi, as a strong new Commission president for the remainder of 1999 and then through 2005 for a regular five-year term. It also spectacularly confirmed the increasing power of the European Parliament in EU politics and ushered in hopes for more transparency and democratic accountability in the European institutions.

effectively exercised (see Box 3.3). The European Court of Justice is composed of one member from each state, again appointed by the executive of each state, and serving a term of six years which may or may not be renewed. While the Court may actually serve as a democratic counterweight to the Council and other Community organs, in the sense that it provides for a separation of powers, it is not of course a popular institution. It is not elected, representative, or accountable. All in all, as Mancini and Keeling argue, the institutional structure of the EU does not present a very democratic picture.

Thus—at least under the original Treaties—power is firmly concentrated in the hands of the governments of the Member States. They possess a virtual monopoly on legislative power, through the Council of Ministers, and hold in addition the exclusive, uncontrolled power to appoint and reappoint the members of the Community's executive and judiciary. If the history of democracy can be seen as a process whereby parliaments wrested power from monarchs, autocrats, and executives, the signing of the Treaty of Rome must to some extent be regarded as a backward step. The willingness of the national parliaments to ratify the Treaty shows how strong the urge for European integration must have been in the 1950s (Mancini and Keeling 1994, 176).

Other aspects of the EU fare no better when judged against the yardstick of democracy. Political parties are weak at the European level. Ties between the national parties and parties in the EP are weak in terms of their organization, financing, and campaigning (Andeweg 1995). Parties do not mobilize constituencies across countries and put forth candidates for public office on a European platform. The interest group system is strong, in the sense that there are hundreds of interest groups represented in Brussels, but these groups mobilize a fraction of the total population. Business is strong, labor is relatively excluded, and the dynamics of European integration possibly even weaken the power of labor at the regional level. The "comitology" system (see Box 3.4) pervades day-to-day decisionmaking, but is largely a system of unaccountable power, what Bobbio calls *sottogoverno*, or subterranean governance. Finally, there is almost no European *agora*, or public forum, within which debates about European public life can take place. Thus, the kind of communicative rationality of which Juergen Habermas speaks, or the public discussion which John Dewey saw as essential to collective problem-solving, is scarcely to be seen on the European landscape (Dewey 1927, 3–36).

THE EU: REPRESENTATION, PARTICIPATION, AND RIGHTS

In the previous section I noted the numerous ways in which the EU can be considered less democratic than the domestic political environment. It is important to remember that the struggle for democracy cannot be reduced to a single variable. It involves many factors: the institutionalization of elections, the growth of political parties, the struggle to include more and more people (non-property holders, women, ethnic and racial minorities) in the electoral process, the expansion of representative institutions, the mobilization of interest factions into interest groups, the building of durable checks and balances, and the establishment of a widespread system of rights to protect citizens from arbitrary exercises of state power. Although it is impossible to examine the EU along each of these

Box 3.4 "Comitology"

"Comitology" refers to the labyrinthine network of committees, usually composed of experts from the member states' national administrations, that supervises the European Commission in the exercise of its delegated powers of implementation. Under these powers, the Commission can enact the highly technical implementing legislation to put technical flesh on the political bones agreed to in primary legislation. Advocates of democratic control of the Union despise the system, formally enshrined in a 1987 Council Decision, for its tendency to work behind closed doors, with neither public nor parliamentary oversight, as well as for the "bewildering array" (Bradley 1992, 693) of procedures by which member states exercise this control. Despite efforts to reduce the incidence of such meetings, it remains high: some 366 committees and 796 experts groups (including 381 of an *ad* hoc nature) met over 1,100 times during the first half of 1999 alone (*European Report*, 28 July 1999). A second Comitology Decision, enacted in June 1999, attempts to improve the transparency of the process by simplifying the procedures and giving the Parliament some control over the implementation of legislation "co-decided" by it and the Council.

dimensions, I have singled out three especially salient aspects of democracy for examination. Below I investigate the EU's performance with regard to representation, participation, and individual rights.

Representation

The main idea behind the importance of representation for democracy is very simple. Unless people can meet in very small groups, such as the workplace, school setting, or town hall, direct, popular democracy is scarcely possible. As a result, authority to represent one's political attitudes is delegated to a formally elected representative who sits in a more broadly elected legislature to debate and decide on key matters of public policy. In large, complex societies, legislative institutions count as a significant conveyor belt between mass opinion and governmental policy-making institutions.

However, the EP is not a supranational version of domestic parliaments. This is so for a variety of reasons, perhaps chief of which is that when the Rome Treaty established the basic institutions of the Community, the drafters did not intend that the EP really be a representative democratic institution. Leaders of the member states very much wanted to retain control of the reins of power, and they rightly saw the legitimacy of the Community institutions as an important issue. The more legitimate the institutions of the Community, the more power and autonomy from national institutions they could rightly claim. As a result, national leaders were not anxious to foster direct elections and a parliament directly linked to the popular will.

Having noted this, it must also be said that the institutions of the Community, once in place, proved to have a dynamic of their own. From the very beginning, members of the European Parliament (MEPs), sometimes with the support of other institutions, lobbied heavily for increased powers and increased representation for the EP. These two things were seen to go together—the greater the democratic legitimacy of the EP, the greater its claims to increased powers. Whether this drive for democracy was the result of MEPs' ideological beliefs or simply the selfish advancement of their institutional interests is beside the point here. As Desmond Dinan puts it:

> The history of the European Parliament is a history of relentless attempts by MEPs to increase their institution's power. Using the argument of democratic unaccountability in the Community—the so-called "democratic deficit"—as a potent weapon, MEPs have sought, especially since the advent of direct elections in 1979, to redress the institutional imbalance between the Commission, Council, and Parliament. With the indispensable assistance of genuinely sympathetic or guilt-ridden governments, Parliament managed in the 1980s and early 1990s to obtain substantially more legislative and supervisory authority (Dinan 1994, 257).

The EP is now a very large body, comprised of 626 members (MEPs) from fifteen different countries. (Article 189 of the Amsterdam Treaty capped future membership at 700 members, whatever the number of states that ultimately accedes to the Union.) Translation is itself a very serious problem since the number of combinations of languages is extremely high. Even though most members of Parliament doubtless know several languages, especially French and English, speaking and listening in the mother tongue are matters of national pride, and humor, wit, irony, and understatement do not travel well across different languages. The size of each country's delegation is roughly proportional to country size. (Some say this reflection is too rough—see Figure 3.2.) Members are now (since 1979) directly elected to the EP, in contrast to the method employed

FIGURE 3.2   Representation in the EP, 1999

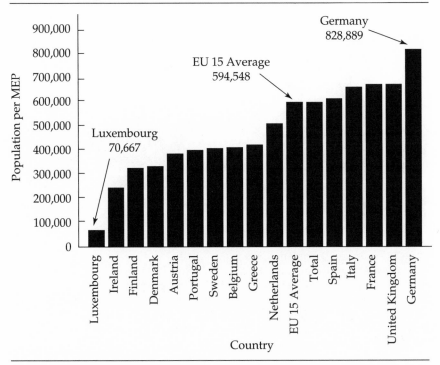

SOURCE: Population figures from Eurostat, URL http://europa.eu.int/en/ comm/eurostat/indic/indic11.htm; author's calculations.

from 1958 to 1979. During that earlier period, representatives were elected to national parliaments and then nominated to sit also in Strasbourg, where the plenary sessions of the EP are held, in effect doing double duty.

Electoral systems across countries may differ greatly in terms of the rules governing who may vote, and the conditions of voting. Five European elections have been held so far (1979, 1984, 1989, 1994, 1999), and they are held at almost the same time in all countries. All European citizens residing in any given country who are over eighteen may vote for EP elections, regardless of nationality. Electoral systems vary, with most of the members using a proportional representation (PR) system whereas the United Kingdom relies on a "first past the post system." The EP is constantly lobbying to get agreement among the countries for a uniform system of voting and electoral laws.

Once members are elected, they spend their time either in Brussels in committee meetings or in Strasbourg, where plenary sessions are held

FIGURE 3.3   Party Groups in the EP, 1999–2004

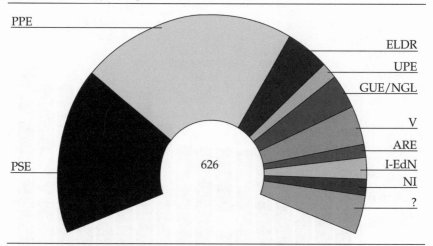

SOURCE: European Parliament, URL
http://www2.europarl.eu.int/election/results/eur15_tab.htm
KEY: PSE = Party of European Socialists; PPE = European People's
Party/European Democrats; ELDR = Liberal, Democratic, and Reform Party;
UPE = Group Union for Europe; GUE/NGL = European United Left/Nordic
Green Left; V = Green Party; ARE = Group of the European Radical Alliance;
I-EdN = Europe of Nations Party; NI = Non-Attached; ? = other parties.

once a month. This in itself is a matter of some controversy in the EU,
since it is not easy to get into or out of Strasbourg. The weekly journeys to
Strasbourg, replete with files and dossiers, make little sense in terms of efficiency and have no obvious democratic argument in their favor either.
The seating and organization of the EP take place by partisan attachment,
rather than territorial (that is, country) membership (see Figure 3.3). Once
in Brussels, elected representatives seek out their closest allies. The three
most prominent groupings are also the parties that have the strongest
showing at the national level: the European People's Party (Christian
Democrats at the national level), the Socialists (Party of European Socialists), and the Liberals (European Liberal Democrats and Reformists). With
new political developments, for example, the appearance of ecological
parties (the Greens) and rightist parties (the *Front National* in France, or
the *Vlaams Blok* in Belgium), representation in the EP changes. All of this
would seem to be quite healthy, with the EU mirroring political cleavages
at the national level and responding to changes in party support with
changes in representation at the European level.

Although the EP has the potential for democratic representation, it currently demonstrates several liabilities. Voter turnout in European elections

TABLE 3.3   Media Coverage of the European Parliament

	1979	1984	1989	1994
Average number of journalists attending sessions	130	156	192	245
Number of TV reports of sessions	NA	394	792	1847
Hours of TV reporting of sessions	57	58	97	325

SOURCE: Corbett 1998, table 3.3, p. 88.

is quite low by national standards, and contrary to expectations, voting rates are declining, with average rates of participation down to just over 58 percent in the 1994 elections (Smith 1995, 4). Decline in electoral turnout refutes the argument that people vote so little because the EU is a young institution, or the EP has so little power. If that were the case, voting rates should go up, whatever the level from which they start. Some of the problems are technical and could be fixed by electoral engineering, for example, the timing of elections could be harmonized so as to take place at similar points in the electoral cycles of all countries. Others may resolve themselves as media attention on the EP increases (see Table 3.3).

However, the problems run much deeper. Turnouts are probably as low as they are not because the EP is not democratic, or because it has few powers, but rather because the choices that are given at the national level are not clearly connected to the operation of parties at the supranational level. Much is made of the fact that members of the EP sit according to political affiliation, with a socialist from Italy sitting next to a French socialist and a Christian Democrat from Germany more likely to sit next to a Christian Democrat from Belgium or the Netherlands. Very little is said about something more fundamental, which is that what the Christian Democratic, Liberal, or Socialist parties do at the national level has little to do with what these corresponding party members do in the EP. If this accusation is true, it amounts to a fundamental disconnection between the national level, where candidates are selected and political issues are formulated, and the European level, where (presumably) policies are made for Europe as a whole. As Andeweg puts it, "For citizens to choose in elections, they must be offered a choice. The menu from which voters may choose is the party system. But for this choice to be meaningful, and for elections to serve as an instrument of political representation, the party system in the parliamentary arena must reflect the party system in the electoral arena. It is this crucial link that is missing in the context of the Euro-elections" (Andeweg 1995, 60).

The natural progression of influence should go from national parties, to transnational party affiliations, to Euro campaigns with candidates nominated by the national and European parties, to European elections, and then, finally, to the making of European legislation by the members of the

European Parliament organized into their transnational groups, all the while informed and disciplined by the national parties. It clearly does not work this way. Instead, the national parties put forth candidates with unclear European credentials, and they most often run on national issues. Euro-elections are thus sometimes thought of as "second-order" elections (Reif and Schmitt 1980). This is true whether the European elections are coterminous with national elections or in-between them. In both cases, it seems that the European elections revolve around national issues and become referenda on the success or failure of the ruling domestic party. What is more, the perception exists that the outcomes of these elections matter little for the national level. This perceived irrelevance encourages people to vote for extreme parties rather than voting strategically with an eye toward making one's vote count.

In short, the linkages between national and European parties are weak, something that cannot be covered up by pointing to the names they use. Ties between the European parties and national parties are weak in the area of campaign finance, issues, political platforms, and party manifestos, and the actual making of consistent policy across domestic and European levels. If the Christian Democratic, Communist, Green, and Socialist party organizations are to mean something, then there should be a strong relationship between the national parties and those operating at the European level. Such ties, however, remain tenuous.

How could the EP, and its representative functions, be strengthened? If the above analysis is correct, a priority would be to strengthen the ties between national and European parties. A first step might be to have candidates nominated by joint bodies composed of both national and European party representatives. In addition, the organizational links between national and European parties should be strengthened, including an integration of finances, candidates, party platforms, and plans on how to govern once a party wins office. Some mechanism must be found to assure that when winning candidates go off to Brussels and Strasbourg, they still remain loyal to the party platform on which they were elected. Party discipline, always problematic even in domestic politics, needs to be enforced between national capitals and Brussels. Exactly what this means in any particular situation may vary, but it could imply a loss of campaign resources and party backing for the next election or the loss of key committee assignments and responsibilities in the EP and so on. While enforcing party discipline across borders may seem a bit "pie-in-the-sky," it is crucial to ground transnational parties in national party structures. Once this link is severed, ordinary citizens have no stake in the outcomes of "European" elections, since the positions espoused by the candidates in the electoral arena bear no definite relation to the behavior of these same individuals in the European Parliament.

A second obvious way to strengthen the EP would be further to increase its legislative powers and responsibilities. The institutional imbalance among the Parliament, Council, and Commission was noted earlier. The Commission enjoys the right of initiative as well as its role as "guardian of the Treaty" while the Council of Ministers has the final word with regard to most legislation. The Court of Justice has clear responsibility for interpreting the Treaty, and increasingly this has come to mean the right to judicial review. Prior to the 1987 SEA, the EP found itself in an institutional no-man's land. For the passage of most legislation, the cliché according to which "the Commission proposes and the Council disposes" was largely accurate, and the Parliament usually had only opinion-giving power. However, with the entry into force of the SEA in 1987, of the Maastricht Treaty in 1993, and the Amsterdam Treaty in 1999, the modest powers of the Parliament have increased tremendously.

The SEA took the first steps in this sense by introducing two new procedures for the adoption of legislation. The "assent procedure" applies to a narrow range of issues (essentially some areas of external relations) and gives the EP an airtight veto over policy changes. The SEA also created a "cooperation procedure" for legislation needed to complete the internal market. While the early stages of this procedure resemble the traditional legislative procedure (Commission proposal, non-binding EP opinion, Council decision), in later stages the EP gains the right to propose amendments that stand a good chance of gaining adoption by the Council. In effect, if the Commission agrees with the EP amendments, it becomes easier for the Council to adopt those amendments (because adoption requires only a qualified majority agreement) than to change or reject them (both of which require unanimity). The cooperation procedure, which was extended to new areas in the 1993 Maastricht Treaty but largely abolished (usually in favor of codecision) at Amsterdam, gave the Parliament substantial "conditional agenda-setting power" (Tsebelis 1994) and enabled it for the first time to exert meaningful legislative influence.

The 1993 Maastricht Treaty extended both the assent and cooperation procedures and, most importantly, created a "codecision procedure" that bestowed additional powers on the EP. This procedure is very complicated and will not be discussed in detail here. What it entails essentially is a limited form of joint legislative power with the Council of Ministers. This power is limited by domain to areas such as the internal market, free movement of persons, rights of establishment, and education, culture, and public health. In effect, if the EP and the Council of Ministers cannot agree on a policy, a conciliation committee is convened which tries to iron out their differences. At the end of the procedure, the EP can veto any policies that the Council might try to impose on it. Skeptics suggested that codecision actually exacerbated the EU's democratic deficit because it replaced the EP's highly-effective "conditional agenda setting power" under cooperation with an absolute veto that it would almost never wish to use (Tsebelis 1997). Further analysis has belied this expectation (Tsebelis et al. 1999), and the 1999 Amsterdam Treaty continued the trend toward increasing EP power by simplifying the procedure and by more than doubling the number of treaty articles that employ it.

Andrew Duff has argued that, because of the codecision procedure, "Maastricht marks the point in the Community's development at which the Parliament became the first chamber of a real legislature. And the Council is obliged to act from time to time like a second legislative chamber rather than a ministerial directorate" (Duff 1994, 31). Whether or not this is entirely accurate, the deeper importance of the extension of EP power may lie in the professionalization of the EP that it demands and in the symbolism of having the EP and the Council meet as equal co-legislators, mutually agreeing to the acts that affect the people of Europe (Jacobs 1997; Scully 1997). If the democratic deficit is defined as the gap between the power of executives operating at the European level, and legislative power and oversight, then steps have been taken to redress the disparity. How successful these steps will be is not yet clear.

Participation

Theoretically at least, a benign ruler could govern on behalf of the masses. If this imaginary ruler were aware of the preferences of the subjects of his or her autocracy, including intensities and trade-offs among different goals, he or she could forge policies designed to fit the needs of the people. Such a system of rule would be "on behalf of" the people while not being "by the people." Politics would be responsive to the wants of the people without involving an active voice of the public in articulating its own concerns. In short, the political system would not be participatory.

Defenders of democracy would be highly skeptical of the above example. It is an interesting thought experiment, they might say, and grudgingly admit that it is a logical possibility, but they would deny that such a situation is either likely to occur—unchecked power corrupts—or desirable even if it occurs. Democrats (small "d") do not take well to paternalism, to having "good" policies bestowed upon them without their asking, nor do they admire a political culture that is inactive, quiescent, and passive. Quite the opposite. As Almond and Verba argued in *The Civic Culture* (1963), democratic theory demands an active citizenry oriented not only to the output side of politics (policies, administrative orders, and procedures) but also to the critical input side (articulating interests, aggregating these interests, and pressing for passage of laws, forming coalitions, public debate).

On what grounds do defenders of participation base their arguments? After all, participation is very costly, particularly if opportunity costs are taken into account. (Opportunity costs measure the foregone uses to which the time could have been put.) Time spent on political participation cuts directly into other pressing daily activities, including working, shopping, cooking meals, driving children to soccer practice, and perhaps reading the newspaper. Even less virtuous activities, such as watching television and drinking beer with friends, compete with the time allocated toward political participation.

Although there are numerous reasons why people should participate, two may be singled out. First, participation is practically crucial for rulers to know what the preferences of the society are. Preferences are complicated; they cannot be divined by rulers or known by direct intuition. They vary by quality, by intensity, and by the rate by which a person will trade off one goal for another. One may be in favor of clean air, but how much is one willing to pay in terms of decreased production or more expensive production technologies to achieve clean air? Lindblom (1977) has argued that authority systems, those that operate with a strong top-down hierarchy, tend to be "all thumbs." They may be able to mobilize a lot of resources but are usually not very good at figuring out what to produce or what people want. The market provides a fine-grained mechanism for figuring out how to allocate resources; it is based on the way people spend their dollars. The political system works with a much less perfectly developed system of competition. It is based on alternative parties rather than firms and individuals chosen on the basis of their vote, their lobbying effort, and other modes of political participation.

A second reason participation is defended as central to democracy is that, quite apart from providing checks on rulers, it creates feelings of efficacy among citizens. Citizens come to have a stake in the political system, identify with it, feel less alienated from it, and gradually acquire feelings of competence and pride. Under the best of circumstances, civic education and tolerance are fostered. We learn about democracy by participating in democratic practices. As Joan Nelson puts it, participation "is both an inherently desirable goal and a means to other goals; it protects liberty, promotes equality, and encourages stability" (Nelson 1987, 104). While she notes that this view may be somewhat idealistic, it is also important to note that without participation, democracy as we know it would not exist. And while there may be participatory excesses, with existing political institutions unable to respond to the "load" of demands made of them, the opposite extreme of an "unburdened" democracy efficiently churning out technically sound policies without bothering to consult people about what they want is equally disturbing.

How does participation take place at the European level? There is no popular vote for anything like a chief executive, a president or a prime minister. The Commission, which initiates and implements, is appointed by the member states, although after the TEU the Parliament has the right to confirm both the individual Commissioners and the president of the Commission. The representatives on the Council of Ministers are of course appointed by the individual chief executives of the member states. Members of the EP are now elected by the citizenry of the member states and EU citizens can vote wherever in the EU they reside. While the Maastricht Treaty created "European citizenship" as a legal concept, there is very little by way of participatory rights for citizens at the European level. As the EP becomes more powerful and more democratic, and as the problems associated with the weak links between national and European parties find solutions (assuming they do), voting in European elections will become more meaningful.

Another way to participate in the EU is through lobbying. One advantage of this approach is that it does not depend upon the establishment of political institutions at the European level provided by treaties. That is, private and public bodies can simply set up an office in Brussels and contact members of the Commission, or Parliament, or Committee of Permanent Representatives and try to persuade them of the value of this or that policy. There are at present over three thousand interest groups located in Brussels, some of them private firms, or agricultural organizations, whereas some are promotional groups or sub-national governments from other countries trying to advance their economic interests. For example, many U.S. state governments have an office in Brussels, as does the U.S. Chamber of Commerce. Justin Greenwood (1997) gives us a good *tour d'horizon* of interest group representation.

> The variety of interests with a stake in European public affairs is vast. It includes firms, professions, employers and labour groups, consumer, cause, social/community, citizen and environmental interests, at European, national, and subnational levels of organization, and territorial interests themselves, such as regional and local government. On a visit to Brussels and Strasbourg it is possible to come across every imaginable type of interest, from multinational firms to aquarium trustees and handwriting analysts, motorcyclists to municipalities, trade unionists to topical campaign groups, craftsmen to citizens and consumers, and bird-lovers to beer-drinkers." (Greenwood 1997, 2)

The specialized nature of pressure groups is certainly a fact of life in Brussels as elsewhere. However, this should not be overstated. There are also large, encompassing, umbrella-like interest groups. Among these are UNICE (the Union of Industries of the European Community), COPA (the

Committee of Professional Agricultural Associations) and ETUC (the European Trade Union Confederation). Also important is EUROCHAMBRES (the Association of European Chambers of Commerce), the ERT (European Roundtable of Industrialists), and AMCHAM-EU (the EU Committee of the American Chamber of Commerce). UNICE is more accurately a true encompassing organization. It is a confederation of 32 national industrial organizations that attempt to represent all of industry (Greenwood 1997, 104). ERT, on the other hand, is a more specialized, indeed exclusive organization, where membership is by invitation only. Members of a select number of influential companies, usually multinational corporations, take part in the important strategic planning that goes on in this group (Cowles 1997, 116). The ERT normally does not get involved in firm-specific matters but rather restricts itself to broad continental or even global matters. The ERT was arguably crucial in inciting the SEA (Cowles 1995).

What are the limitations of European participatory democracy? First, with regard to interest group participation, we should note the unequal nature of the representation. Business is heavily and effectively represented while labor and consumers much less so. Justin Greenwood reports data showing that two-thirds of all groups headquartered in Brussels are business organizations (1997, 10). Furthermore, large firms with highly mobile capital and low asset-specificity gain more than smaller firms that have fixed capital or capital that cannot be easily shifted to another sector. As predicted by Mancur Olson (1965), concentrated interests do better than large, diffuse interests. Quite apart from the resources at their disposal, concentrated interests have less difficulty organizing. Large, diffuse groups such as consumers face nightmarish problems of collective organization.

While business is unquestionably over-represented, the Commission sometimes fosters groups that might not otherwise be included. For example, it has been active in trying to create a network of groups in the area of social policy, particularly with regard to the rights of women at work and, more broadly, in the marketplace. It also substantially funds numerous environmental non-governmental organizations (NGOs). If E. E. Schattschneider is right that politics is about the mobilization of bias so as to "enlarge the scope of public conflict," then the Commission is doing a service by activating groups that might not, for collective action reasons, organize effectively or at all (Schattschneider 1960, 35).

A second limitation of the participatory structure of the EU, centering heavily on interest groups, is that interest group politics, if not embedded within a larger political structure that includes parties, legislatures, and popularly chosen executives, leads to some political maladies. In the EU there is an absence of larger participatory structures through which interest group demands can be channeled, compromised, and forged into common policy positions. In short, if there is a weak party structure, there will be a weak process of interest aggregation. Individual interest groups will confront Community political institutions on their own and naturally try to cut their own deals. Within a domestic polity, these interest groups would first have to confront the interests of others, that is, the opposing interests, and try to achieve some form of compromise before their positions reach policymaking institutions.

Why worry about all of this, some might ask? What difference does it make if interest groups go directly to the Commission or the EP instead of working their way toward the top through a party structure? One answer is that democratic legitimacy suffers as a result of the way interest groups dominate the European system. There is nothing unnatural about groups wanting to advance their own interests. However, the argument is that unless these interests come together in some comprehensive way, unless parties or some other institution form coalitions based on aggregations of these interest groups, and unless these coalitions compete with one another through public debate, people are not likely to be very interested in what goes on, except of course in their own private bailiwick. The public consequences of the sum of their private activities will be suboptimal.

Rights and the Rule of Law

Periodic elections, broad, encompassing political parties, representative legislatures, and a healthy society in terms of interest groups and civic associations are what we normally focus on when we think of democracy. However, the extension of rights to individuals, guaranteed by the state, even against the fluctuating tides of public opinion, can also be seen as an important part of the democratic process. Yet, the spread of rights and their entrenchment in constitutions, so that their enforcement depends not just on the whim of the ruler but on some more deeply institutionalized process, is not necessarily related to other dimensions of democracy in a one-for-one manner. A ruler could be responsive to democratic participation (to votes, to preferences for certain policies) and not be tightly constrained by a system of laws, and a dictator could be very undemocratic and still work within a framework of laws. In other words, there is a difference between sheer personal rule no matter how democratic, and rule by law, no matter how undemocratic. The idea of the modern democratic state is one in which there is both impersonal rule ("a nation of laws and not of people") and democracy, in the sense of institutionalized connections between rulers and ruled.

We can think of rights as claims people make for certain conditions, benefits, and safeguards regardless of their position in the market or society. The first and most basic kinds of rights can be thought of as "negative rights" in the sense that they constitute rights to be free from interference by political authorities. The attempt in the seventeenth century, following the end of the Thirty Years War in 1648, to carve out a private space for the practice of religion, is an example of the historical creation of a right to be free from state intrusion. Freedom from government interference of any kind (arbitrary arrests, searches and seizures, torture) would fall into this category of negative freedoms. Participation rights (to vote, seek, and hold office) and rights of speech and political expression would constitute another category. Still a third category, far from universally accepted even among countries called democratic, would be social rights, for example, housing rights, medical care rights, unemployment insurance rights. The general idea is that once these rights are instituted, they are overriding, in the sense that popular majorities cannot decide to deny them. If, for example, a society has instituted the right of everyone to a fair and speedy trial by jury, then a group of people, indeed even the entire nation, cannot decide to imprison or execute someone summarily because they think he or she is guilty. Rights trump preferences and provide a check on the will of majorities. This is one of the essential differences between a pure democracy and a republic. In a pure democracy, decisions are made by majority rule. In a republic, certain basic rights are entrenched and cannot be overridden by a majority decision.

In the preceding sections of this chapter, I have emphasized the limitations of the EU in terms of the democratic nature of its institutions and practices. The Parliament is weak (though becoming stronger), the shift of powers from national capitals to Brussels has not been compensated by an increase in either domestic or supranational legislative powers, the party system is cut off from the national parties, and the interest group system, while strong, is also biased. But there is another aspect of democracy to pursue here, and that is the capacity of individuals to "vindicate their rights in judicial proceedings" (Mancini and Keeling 1994, 184). In the next to last section of this chapter, I consider the possibility of the building up of a system of rights through judicial activity. To what extent are individuals provided rights as a result of their position as European citizens, apart from and beyond the rights to which they are entitled on the basis of national citizenship? And to what extent has the ECJ been instrumental in the provision of these rights?

At the outset, the ECJ might seem to be an unlikely candidate for the expansion of democratic rights. It is a small body (composed of fifteen members at present), it conducts its proceedings in secret (even more so than the Council of Ministers), does not publish dissenting opinions, and is of course not popularly elected. In short, it is a small, elite, and secretive body of lawyers. In comparison to other ways of improving on democracy in the EU, such as expanding the powers of the EP, increasing the transparency of the Council of Ministers, strengthening political parties, the role of the Court would seem limited.

In addition, before the ECJ could become the vehicle for the expansion of rights, there were a few not so minor obstacles to overcome. The first obstacle was so huge that it prevented everyone from even considering the potential of an international court in this area. To put the point simply, the basic legal document that founded the EU, the Rome Treaty, was an international agreement—not a constitution. The difference is fundamental.

A constitution sets forth a set of rights and responsibilities for individuals. As a result of these constitutional provisions, there are concrete duties (such as serving in the armed forces, paying taxes) as well as rights (voting, trial by jury, free speech) for which individuals have judicial recourse, that is, the political system is duty-bound to provide remedies through the courts. No remedies means no enforceable rights, which effectively means no rights at all. A treaty, by contrast, is a compact among states, a legal agreement entered into by states to secure certain ends. It is not that treaties have no standing in law; they clearly do. Neither is it the case that international law is weak because there is no enforcement mechanism. Compliance is not universally problematic, even though there is no supranational Leviathan. The main problem, from the standpoint of the expansion of rights spearheaded by an international institution such as the ECJ, lies quite simply in the fact that treaties bind states and not individuals. Thus, if the job of the Court is to interpret the Treaty, its task is to draw out the content for the obligations of states. As Mancini (a former judge on the ECJ at present) and Keeling put it, the term "Community" of which the Rome Treaty spoke, referred to a community of states, not of individuals (Mancini and Keeling 1994, 176). Individuals, firms, and other non-state actors had no legal status.

Furthermore, the Treaty of Rome lacks any serious statement of individual rights, and it provides very little by way of enforcement of those scattered rights that do exist. Article 173 of the Treaty allows individuals to bring actions before the Court only for actions which affect them individually and directly. For example, if a lawyer felt that her or his "freedom to move" were restricted by laws on the credentials required for lawyers in another member state, there would be no right to bring the case before the Court, since such restrictions, no matter how discriminatory, would affect all lawyers in the same way. Finally, there are "no circumstances in which an individual may sue a member state directly in the Court of Justice" (Mancini and Keeling 1994, 182).

Thirdly, even if the Community Treaties provided rights for individuals, the relationship between domestic and international law is unclear. Suppose domestic and international laws were to conflict. Which law would govern? This is a more complicated question than it may at first seem. Many domestic legal systems simply incorporate international law into the domestic legal order. In parliamentary systems, Acts of parliament are supreme, and later Acts of parliament are controlling in the face of conflicting prior Acts. Thus, in a parliamentary system, any international treaty obligation can be overridden simply by a later Act of parliament, a doctrine known as *lex posteriori*. The meta-norm (the higher-level norm) that the more recent rule applies works in favor of domestic parliaments in that treaty law can be overturned by a simple Act of parliament.

Now altering this state of affairs, which recognizes that states are the essential actors in the international system, and that rights and responsibilities are for individual states to decide in accordance with their own constitutions, is no small matter. State sovereignty is an organizing principle of the state system. States are legally equal to one another, can make agreements with one another, and have the authority to set up distinctive patterns of rights and responsibilities internally.

In Chapter 2, I referred to the process by which the ECJ altered the Rome Treaty as "constitutionalization" (Mancini 1991; Stone Sweet 1995). This awkward term describes a process by which an international treaty, a compact among states, becomes relevant for individuals within those states. Constitutionalization is "the process by which the EC treaties evolved from a set of legal arrangements binding upon sovereign states, into a vertically integrated legal regime conferring judicially enforceable rights and obligations on all legal persons and entities, public and private, within EC territory" (Stone Sweet 1995, 1).

How did such a revolution come about, especially since it is hard to imagine that the member states would have gone along with it? If we simplify greatly, the answer is that the ECJ progressively made the Treaties relevant to individuals, firms, and other private and public actors. To do so, it first had to place the legal status of individuals on a firm foundation. As indicated in Chapter 2, the historic cases had to do with direct effect (the *Van Gend* case, 1963) and superiority (the *Costa* case, 1964).

Before the *Van Gend* case, it was possible for member states to sue one another. In addition, the European Commission could bring infringement proceedings against individual member states for non-compliance with Community law. But individuals had no legal standing. They could not sue another individual for breaches of Community law, or sue their employer, or bring legal proceedings against a public authority in their home country. The *Van Gend* case addressed precisely this legal gap and started the process by which an ordinary citizen could go to court to seek a remedy in the face of a perceived lack of enforcement of Community law. Since 1963 and this landmark case, the Court has elaborated its case law and has extended the doctrine of direct effect from Treaty provisions to

FIGURE 3.4   The Three Pillar European Union, 1993 Maastricht Treaty

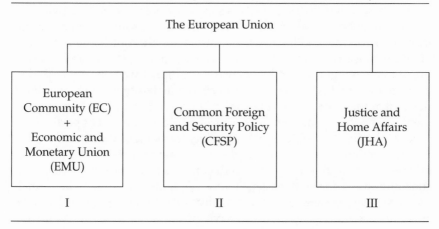

directives and other secondary legislation. When domestic laws were out of line with European law, the ECJ sought to narrow that gap, putting legal pressure on domestic parliaments and courts to bring national laws up to the European standard. Thus, what started out as a thin wedge of constitutional protections (based on selected portions of the Treaty) extended to other areas.

The ECJ is just one Community institution, and its role and powers are also subject to the control of other institutions, such as the Council of Ministers. For example, when the Maastricht Treaty was negotiated, the two new pillars—Common Foreign and Security Policy (CFSP) and Justice and Home Affairs (JHA)—were put outside the jurisdictional scope of the Court of Justice (see Figure 3.4). Only the "first pillar" (comprising the old European Community, plus EMU) remained under direct ECJ supervision. Whereas the Amsterdam Treaty integrates much of the third pillar into the European Community proper (thus placing it directly under ECJ supervision), the CFSP remains largely outside of Court control. It is important to bear in mind that the Court of Justice can only adjudicate on the basis of legal texts, and these legal texts are the various treaties that constitute the Community system. Of course, within these boundaries, the Court may take a restrained or an expansive view of things, corresponding to strict construction versus more liberal interpretation of the U.S. Constitution.

Having made these limitations clear, the Court has made remarkable progress. It has done so not only in areas where one might expect it, such as free movement and competition, but also in places where progress has been exceedingly slow and painful in the other institutions. As outlined in Chapter 2, the Council of Ministers and the Commission made relatively little progress on the social policy front, despite the fact that Jacques Delors, who was president of the Commission from 1985 to 1995, was a French Socialist who attached considerable priority to movement toward a common social policy. The 1989 "Social Charter," which was to be the accompaniment to the completion of the internal market by the end of 1992, never really amounted to much. By contrast, the ECJ, relying on rather flimsy Treaty provisions, managed to make considerable headway in many areas.

The Court's jurisprudence also brought about some important procedural changes. Among these changes were the upgrading of domestic laws in light of the European standard (interpreting such laws more rigorously when the European standard is higher) and the rewriting of domestic laws so as to make them conform to European Treaty law or secondary legislation. For example, both the Equal Pay Act and the Sex Discrimination Act of the United Kingdom were amended so as to bring them more in line with European standards, as provided by the Equal Pay Directive (1975) and the Equal Treatment Directive (1976). The Sex Discrimination Act of the U.K. was redrafted so as to narrow exceptions about pregnancy, retirement, and protective legislation (Caporaso and Jupille 2000, 32).

The institutionalization of rights is a cornerstone of democracy. Without clearly specified rights, backed up by courts, the individual is powerless against arbitrary governmental actions. There can be little doubt that the ECJ has made progress in establishing individual rights at the European level. In Chapter 2, I examined in some detail how these rights came to life in the area of equal pay and equal treatment. These rights are part of a larger pattern in which individuals are acquiring legal standing in front of the European Court. In the section below, I examine an emerging area of cooperation where democracy has not fared so well, monetary cooperation.

AN EXAMPLE: MONETARY POLICY AND DEMOCRACY

One of the newest and most important areas of competence of the EU concerns monetary policy. Since this policy arena has important consequences for EU nationals, it is relevant to ask about the effectiveness of democratic controls. The ability to coin and print money, to incur government debt, and to determine interest rates and exchange rates are key powers that governments have with respect to the economy. These activities are important in their own right but also because they are related to other macroeconomic conditions such as inflation and unemployment.

Indeed, the supply of money is often taken as a reliable predictor of inflation. Thus, it is no surprise that when a new state forms, one of its first challenges is to devise a monetary policy of its own. Monetary policy is at the core of national sovereignty (Sandholtz 1993).

However, the modern world presents some dilemmas regarding the meaning of democratic control over monetary policy. The most obvious dilemma has to do with the meaning of sovereign control in an environment of international interdependence. Trade dependence among EU members is very high and, as we have seen, the concentration of this trade within the EU has been growing rapidly. Integration in capital markets is also high and growing. As Garrett notes, traders operating around the clock can move huge amounts of money around the globe nearly instantaneously (Garrett 1998, 792). Goodman and Pauly demonstrate that the integration of the financial sector, particularly short-term movements of money, has exploded in the last several decades (Goodman and Pauly 1993, 57).

As trade and financial flows among countries increase, national policy instruments have less effect. For example, imagine that Germany wants to heat up its economy, and that it chooses the traditional route—increase of its money supply—to do so. By making more money available, people will spend more, and this will by definition increase demand. However, since Germany is an open economy, some of the increased purchasing power will "leak" abroad in the form of demand for more imports. By the same logic, if France tries to administer high-spending policies by increasing the benefits attached to the welfare state, it can do so only at the serious risk of incurring inflation, and this in turn will put pressure on its exchange rate. As spending increases, inflation will occur, thus making it harder to export French goods and easier to import the goods of other countries. Thus, there will be pressure for devaluation of the French franc to make French goods more competitive.

In principle, countries may retain full sovereign control over monetary policy, but in practice, they will not be able to achieve their goals in isolation from one another. Achieving economic goals will increasingly require cooperation. The first dilemma involves a trade-off between sovereign control over money and ability to achieve national economic goals. This dilemma is indirectly relevant to the theme of this chapter in that democracy assumes that states are capable of acting on behalf of their citizens.

The second dilemma is directly relevant. We can put this dilemma simply. The making of monetary policy requires expertise (which suggests delegation of the task to experts), whereas democracy requires some public input, representation, and accountability. The move to Economic and Monetary Union (EMU) has decided in favor of expertise and independence, at least for the time being. I will explore this choice in more detail.

Dilemma Between Interdependence
and Sovereign Policymaking

The Treaty of Rome did not set out procedures for monetary integration. Perhaps Euro-enthusiasts hoped for eventual monetary integration, but at the time (during the 1950s), integration in this sector seemed premature. Instead, EEC officials and national leaders concentrated on creation of the free trade area and the construction of the common agricultural policy (CAP) during the first decade. However, the very successes in agriculture and in trade made for higher levels of interdependence, which in turn made the control of money across borders more important. Instability of currencies, both within Europe and between EEC members and the United States, created havoc with the pricing system in agriculture (Verdun 1999, 6). Thus, it was no accident that Pierre Werner, Prime Minister of Luxembourg, put forward his initial proposal to move toward some form of monetary unification in January 1968. It was the forthcoming deadlines with regard to elimination of internal tariffs in July 1968, along with the effect of currency changes on agricultural prices, that prompted Werner's proposals (Cameron 1998, 195).

Throughout the seventies and eighties, levels of interdependence continued to grow, and these trends were only reinforced by the passage of the Single European Act in the mid-eighties. The SEA broadened the scope of integration, and carried the idea of interdependence from trade to the movement of productive factors, including labor and capital. The SEA anticipated that, by the end of 1992, the internal market among the member states would be substantially complete. If this were to come about, it would exert even stronger pressures on national currencies, since any country could undo an advantage enjoyed by another simply by varying the value of its currency. In a sense, the manipulation of the value of a national currency could substitute for its tariffs. The entire logic of the internal market seemed to require a mechanism to control, and perhaps to eliminate, movements in exchange rates.

Those who drafted the SEA recognized the connection between the market in goods and monetary policy (Cameron 1998, 196; Verdun 1999, 310). The preamble to the SEA pointed out that "progressive realization of economic and monetary union" was one of the long-standing objectives of the EU (Cameron 1998, 196). By the late eighties, Jacques Delors established a group of experts to outline a scheme for economic and monetary union, as part of the overall negotiations for the Treaty on European Union (TEU). This group consisted of central bank presidents and independent experts. The Delors Report called for a single currency—thus eliminating exchange rate volatility—and a European Central Bank (ECB), consisting of a central monetary authority modeled along lines of the German *Bundesbank* and the national banks.

The Delors Report was largely accepted and was reflected in the TEU. The TEU called for monetary integration in three stages. The first stage called for the establishment of free capital movements among the member states, a condition that had existed formally at least since 1988, when capital controls were abolished (Cameron 1998, 196). During stage two the European central banks were to monitor national monetary policies and coordinate them. Also, permissible variations in exchange rates were to be narrowed. Stage three called for "irrevocably fixed" exchange rates, and implied a common currency. In this stage, full authority for monetary policy was to be transferred to EU institutions (Dinan 1994, 422).

In January 1999 stage three began with eleven of the fifteen EU member states; Greece, Sweden, the United Kingdom, and Denmark did not join. Thus, centralized monetary policy is now the law of the land in Europe. The significance of this transfer of authority to the supranational level is difficult to exaggerate. As one authority put it,

> EMU implies no less than the transfer of macroeconomic policymaking . . . from the national to the European level. The most important aspect of EMU is that exchange rates between national currencies will be "irrevocably" fixed and then replaced by [a single European currency, the Euro]. Consequently, monetary policy will no longer be conducted on a national basis. National central banks will lose their autonomy, and adjustments will no longer be possible through exchange rates (Kaufmann 1995, 267–268).

The EU has dealt with the dilemma between international interdependence and ability to achieve economic goals unilaterally by delegating authority to make economic policy to supranational institutions. We have seen that interdependence, particularly capital mobility, undermines the autonomous pursuit of economic goals and encourages states to coordinate their policies regarding inflation, interest rates, budget deficits, and exchange rates. EU member states have resolved the tension between interdependence and autonomy by creating a supranational authority (the European Central Bank) higher than the states themselves. This is especially clear with the introduction of the third stage of EMU involving the creation of the single currency (the Euro) and the delegation of monetary policymaking authority to the ECB.

However, the movement to monetary integration creates a largely unaccountable economic power, the ECB. What implications does this have for the democratic nature of the EU?

Dilemma Between Democracy and Expertise

I have mentioned that the Delors Report, largely adopted as part of the TEU, was written by a committee of experts—twelve central bank governors, two commissioners, and three independent experts—whose collective bias was without doubt price stability (controlling inflation). Other economic goals, such as creation of jobs and reduction in the disparities of income, were not addressed. In objective terms, an unemployment rate of 11 percent to 12 percent would seem to be a problem. Yet, it was given virtually no attention by the committee of experts nor did a concern for jobs make an appearance in the convergence criteria by which countries were assessed fit or unfit for EMU membership.

Further, the way in which EMU is designed to operate is not democratic. There is no mechanism for public input, the ECB is insulated from broad political pressures, and there are only very weak mechanisms for accountability and control. As Berman and McNamara argue, "the officials who make these decisions will not have to answer to the publics whose jobs and quality of life hang in the balance. The bankers will not even have to give Europeans much basic information on how and why bank decisions are made" (Berman and McNamara 1999, 2). Remarkably, Wim Duisenberg, the first head of the ECB, remarked that while it was normal for politicians to inquire about the operations of central banks and to make suggestions, it would be "abnormal" if those suggestions were listened to (Berman and McNamara 1999, 6). In short, the EMU, and the ECB, do not come out well when measured against most standards of democratic performance, including representation, information, transparency, participation, accountability, and control.

Advocates of central bank independence point out that central banks have a good record in terms of fighting inflation and in terms of economic performance in general. The inflation link seems justified but, beyond this, the record is unclear. In a major study of the relationship between economic performance and central bank independence, the authors failed to find a link between bank independence and economic growth (Alesina and Summers 1988). In addition, quite apart from the results produced, democracy is also about the process by which things get done. Advocates of democracy argue that a dictator may be able to get the trains to run on time, but that is not the only thing that counts. It is also important how a society makes decisions about its collective life.

In terms of the democratic dilemma, that is, the choice between the organization of monetary policy in democratic terms versus the independent, expert authorities, clearly the trade-off has been more in the direction of independence and expertise. There are other ways (other than a bank outside public control) to organize economic policymaking in an interdependent world, and some of these alternatives emphasize greater political control. The French have been particularly vocal about creating some form of "political counterpart" to balance and guide the power of the ECB. Both President Jacques Chirac and the French Minister of Finance, Jean Arthuis, called in 1997 for some form of economic government, composed perhaps of representatives of countries who have moved into the third stage commencing in 1999 (Cameron 1998, 214). These representatives could be drawn from the Ministries of Finance of the member states and could constitute an ongoing political body to check and guide the experts in the Bank.

Perhaps the ECB will continue to operate as it is presently designed, pursuing its central goal of controlling inflation. This may imply an acceptance of low growth, high unemployment, and price stability in the years ahead. If so, this may affect the legitimacy of the EU. It is accepted that economic performance affects political support within countries. Citizens have come to expect that politicians deliver the goods economically. What is often not recognized is that low growth and high unemployment also diminish the degree of public support for the EU as an institution. As unemployment goes up, since 1991 at least, political support for membership in the EU goes down (Cameron 1998, 211).

Economic interdependence in Western Europe is very deep and broad. It cuts across many areas of life, including trade, movement of labor and capital, integration of financial markets, tourism, and entertainment. Thus, when governments attempt to deal with problems arising from a conflict between interdependence and autonomous pursuit of goals, they often choose in favor of interdependence. However, the choice of institutional form of cooperative decisionmaking, whether the institutions are demo-cratic or not, is much more open. Thus, the choice to organize monetary union along nondemocratic lines is likely to be contested in the years ahead.

CONCLUSION

As I have argued in this chapter, democracy implies many different things, and all good things do not necessarily go together. To Madisonians, institutionally entrenched checks and balances represent critical bulwarks against the corrupting influences of concentrated power. To constitutionalists, rule of law is central. To populists, it is the influence of the people, operating as directly as possible through votes, referenda, and public debate. To critics of mass society, who recognize the difficulties of organizing people who live in large nation-states, strong, responsible party government may be the answer. And to almost everyone, strong representative institutions are almost by definition important for democratic institutions to take hold.

The EU has done poorly on some dimensions of democracy. Legislative power remains concentrated, and not in the hands of a legislature, but in the hands of a Council of appointed national ministers. Secrecy is the rule rather than the exception not only where one expects it (Courts) but also where it is not usually judged appropriate (legislative institutions, committees, working groups). A gap between the power balance that exists at the national level and the corresponding institutional balance at the European level is wide and shows only modest signs of closing.

On the other hand, democratic forces have made some advances. If the rule of law is allowed as an indicator of democracy, then the ECJ has made important headway. The EP is now (since 1979) directly elected, and its legislative influence has increased through the Single European Act, the Maastricht Treaty, and the Amsterdam Treaty. Political parties, while still hampered by many weaknesses, have at least moved somewhat to correct the many problems that face them, though here the work to be done is considerable.

Of one thing we can be sure, namely, there is a European public in John Dewey's sense, a group of people considerably affected by international transactions but not a party to those transactions. A European market society has been created at the regional level. These European market transactions are not self-contained, creating externalities in the same way that market transactions within national societies do. Dewey saw the germ of the state in the distinction between private and public. As society moves from the polar extreme of pure individualism, where private individuals work and stay mostly to themselves, to an integrated society characterized by a complex division of labor, they will also move from a situation where external consequences are small and exceptional to one where they are large and routine. As we approach the latter end of the continuum, public consequences of market activity will be salient, and regulation of these consequences will be called for. In a supranational organization where the constituent members are democratically organized, pressure will no doubt emerge for the democratic control of transnational activities.

REFERENCES

Alesina, Alberto, and Lawrence H. Summers. 1988. "Central Bank Independence and Macroeconomic Performance: Some Comparative Evidence." *Journal of Money, Credit, and Banking* 25 (May):151–162.

Almond, Gabriel A., and Sidney Verba. 1963. *The Civic Culture*. Princeton, N.J.: Princeton University Press.

Andeweg, Rudy. 1995. "The Reshaping of National Party Systems." In *The Crisis of Representation in Europe*, edited by Jack Hayward. London and Portland, Ore.: Frank Cass.

Berman, Sheri, and Kathleen R. McNamara. 1999. "Bank on Democracy," *Foreign Affairs* 78, no. 2 (March/April):2–8.

Bobbio, Norberto. 1987. *The Future of Democracy: A Defense of the Rules of the Game.* Minneapolis, Minn.: University of Minnesota Press.

Bowles, Samuel, and Herbert Gintis. 1986. *Democracy and Capitalism: Property, Community, and the Contradictions of Modern Social Thought.* New York: Basic Books.

Bradley, Kieran St. Clair. 1992. "Comitology and the Law: Through a Glass, Darkly." *Common Market Law Review* 29, no. 4 (August): 693–721.

Cameron, David. 1992. "The 1992 Initiative: Causes and Consequences." In *Europolitics: Institutions and Policymaking in the 'New' European Community*, edited by Alberta M. Sbragia. Washington, D.C.: The Brookings Institution.

_____. 1998. "Creating Supranational Authority in Monetary and Exchange-Rate Policy: The Sources and Effects of EMU." In *European Integration and Supranational Governance*, edited by Wayne Sandholtz and Alec Stone Sweet. Oxford: Oxford University Press.

Caporaso, James A., and Joseph Jupille. 2000. "The Europeanization of Gender Equality Policy and Domestic Structural Change." To appear in *Transforming Europe: Europeanization and Domestic Change*, edited by Maria Green Cowles, James A. Caporaso, and Thomas Risse. Ithaca, N.Y.: Cornell University Press.

Corbett, Richard. 1998. *The European Parliament's Role in Closer EU Integration.* London: Macmillan.

Cowles, Maria Green. 1995. "Setting the Agenda for the New Europe: the ERT and EC 1992." *Journal of Common Market Studies* 33, no. 4:501–526.

_____. 1997. "Organizing Industrial Coalitions: A Challenge for the Future? In *Participation and Policy Making in the European Union*, edited by Helen Wallace and Alasdair R. Young. Oxford: Clarendon Press.

Dewey, John. 1927. *The Public and Its Problems.* Chicago: The Swallow Press.

Dinan, Desmond. 1994. *An Ever Closer Union?* Boulder, Colo.: Lynne Rienner Publishers.

Duff, Andrew. 1994. "The Main Reforms." In *Maastricht and Beyond: Building the European Union*, edited by Andrew Duff et al. London and New York: Routledge.

European Report. 28 July 1999.

Friedman, Milton. 1962. *Capitalism and Freedom.* Chicago: University of Chicago Press.

Friedrich, Carl J. 1937. *Constitutional Government and Democracy: Nature and Development.* New York: Harper.

Garrett, Geoffrey. 1998. "Global Markets and National Politics: Collision Course or Virtuous Circle?" *International Organization* 52, no. 4 (Autumn):787–824.

Golub, Jonathan. 1999. "In the Shadow of the Vote: Decision Making in the European Community." *International Organization* 53, no. 4 (Autumn):733–764.

Goodman, John B., and Louis W. Pauly. 1993. "The Obsolescence of Capital Controls? Economic Management in an Age of Global Markets." *World Politics* 46, no. 1 (October):50–82.

Greenwood, Justin. 1997. *Representing Interests in the European Union.* New York: St. Martin's Press.

Jacobs, Francis. 1997. "Legislative Co-Decision: A Real Step Forward?" Presented at the Fifth Biennial Meeting of the European Community Studies Association, May 29–June 1, Seattle, Wash.

Kaufmann, Hugo M. 1995. "The Importance of Being Independent: Central Bank Independence and the European System of Central Banks." In *The State of the European Union*, vol. 3, *Building a European Polity?*, edited by Carolyn Rhodes and Sonia Mazey. Boulder, Colo.: Lynne Rienner Publishers.

Lane, Robert E. 1991. "Self-Attribution: Market Influences." In *The Market Experience*. Cambridge, England: Cambridge University Press.

Lindblom, Charles E. 1977. *Politics and Markets*. New York: Basic Books, Inc.

Mancini, G. Federico. 1991. "The Making of a Constitution for Europe." In *The New European Community: Decisionmaking and Institutional Change*, edited by Robert O. Keohane and Stanley Hoffman. Boulder, Colo.: Westview Press.

Mancini, G. Federico, and David T. Keeling. 1994. "Democracy and the European Court of Justice." *The Modern Law Review* 57, no. 2 (March):175–190.

Mazey, Sonia, and Jeremy Richardson. 1993. "Introduction: Transference of Power, Decision Rules, and Rules of the Game." In *Lobbying in the European Community*, edited by Sonia Mazey and Jeremy Richardson. Oxford, England: Oxford University Press.

Nelson, Joan. 1987. "Political Participation." In *Understanding Political Development*, edited by Myron Weiner and Samuel P. Huntington. Boston, Mass.: Little, Brown and Co.

Olson, Mancur Jr. 1965. *The Logic of Collective Action*. New York: Schocken Books.

Putnam, Robert, with Robert Leonardi and Raffaella Y. Nanetti. 1993. *Making Democracy Work*. Princeton, N.J.: Princeton University Press.

Reif, Karlheinz, and H. Schmitt. 1980. "Nine Second-Order National Elections—a Conceptual Framework for the Analysis of European Election Results." *European Journal of Political Research* 8, no. 1 (March):3–44.

Sandholtz, Wayne. 1993. "Choosing Union: Monetary Politics and Maastricht." *International Organization* 47, no. 1 (Winter):1–39.

Sandholtz, Wayne, and Alec Stone Sweet, eds. 1998. *European Integration and Supranational Governance*. Oxford, England: Oxford University Press.

Sbragia, Alberta M. 1993. "The European Community: A Balancing Act." *Publius* 23, no. 3 (Summer):23–38.

Schattschneider, E. E. 1960. *The Semisovereign People: A Realist's View of Democracy in America*. New York: Holt, Rinehart, and Winston.

Scully, Roger M. 1997. "Policy Influence and Participation in the European Parliament." *Legislative Studies Quarterly* 22, no. 2 (May):233–252.

Smith, Julie. 1995. *Voice of the People: The European Parliament in the 1990s*. London: Royal Institute of International Affairs.

Spruyt, Hendrik. 1994. *The Sovereign State and Its Competitors: An Analysis of Systems Change*. Princeton, N.J.: Princeton University Press.

Stone Sweet, Alec. 1995. "Constitutional Dialogues in the European Community." European University Institute Working Paper, RSC no. 95/38. Badia Fiesolana, San Domenico, Italy.

Streeck, Wolfgang. 1997. "Industrial Citizenship Under Regime Competition: The Case of the European Works Councils." *Journal of European Public Policy* 4, no. 4: 643–664.

Teasdale, Anthony. 1993. "The Life and Death of the Luxembourg Compromise." *Journal of Common Market Studies* 31, no. 4 (December):567–579.

Tsebelis, George. 1994. "The Power of the European Parliament as a Conditional Agenda Setter." *American Political Science Review* 88, no. 1 (March):128–142.

_____. 1997. "Maastricht and the Democratic Deficit." *Aussenwirtschaft* 52, nos. 1 and 2:38–56.

Tsebelis, George, *et al.* 1999. "Legislative Procedures in the European Union: An Empirical Analysis." Presented at the Sixth Biennial Conference of the European Community Studies Association (ECSA), June 2–5, Pittsburgh, Penn.

Verdun, Amy. 1999. "The Role of the Delors Committee in the Creation of EMU: An Epistemic Community?" *Journal of European Public Policy* 6, no. 2: 308–328.

"Veto Mania." *Economist.* 18 February 1985, 48–49.

Weiler, J.J.H. 1994. "A Quiet Revolution: The European Court of Justice and Its Interlocutors." *Comparative Political Studies* 26, no. 4 (January):510–534.

Williams, Shirley. 1991. "Sovereignty and Accountability in the European Community." In *The New European Community* edited by Robert O. Keohane and Stanley Hoffmann. Boulder, Colo.: Westview Press.

FOUR

□　□　□

Dilemmas of the External Relations
of the European Union

In this chapter, I describe some of the main problems and prospects of the external relations of the European Union. I will focus on three themes, each one giving rise to an important dilemma. These three themes have to do with Europe's relationship to the outside world (open versus closed), the relationship between widening and deepening, and Europe's capacity to construct a Common Foreign and Security Policy (CFSP) without member states relinquishing their sovereignty.

The first thing to note is the double meaning of *external* when one is speaking of the EU. The term can refer first to the foreign relations and activities of the member states, or to the relations of the EU considered as an entity, to other state and non-state actors around the world. People freely speak of Europe and "Europe's role in the world" as if the component member states acted in some collective capacity. One hears of "Europe's role in the Uruguay Round of tariff negotiations" or "Europe and the Lomé countries" without thinking about it. This collective representation of Europe's member states entails a remarkable cognitive shift (Rhodes 1998). Before World War II, Europe was indeed scarcely more than a geographical or cultural expression. Now the term *Europe* suggests a coherent unit acting in a collective capacity.

The distinction between inside and outside is fundamental to the domestic-international divide. The identity of a country, its political institutions and often its way of life, are bound up with the capacity to demarcate a geographical zone within which its own laws apply. Indeed, a state may be defined as a territorially exclusive zone of legitimate authority. But what if a group of states, all with the capacity to claim authoritative rule within an area, starts to delegate some aspects of decision-making and authority to the supranational level? What if states look to a more encompassing level to solve problems, fuel their identities, and conduct their everyday business? In other words, what happens when a group of states, in their interactions with one another, starts to resemble the individual units of which the group is composed? This is essentially what happens when the EU is considered as an emerging federation, or a polity within which politics and policymaking occur just as within any single nation-state.

The organization of people into nation-states has led to two major wars in Europe within the twentieth century. Millions of lives were lost during these two world wars. World War II left Europe in a shambles: It was economically devastated, with much of its industrial capacity and infrastructure destroyed, and even the political capacity of many states was under severe challenge from both the left and the right. European recovery had to take place, but it had to do so by a method which did not merely put the old states back on their feet, ready to go to war once again. There were certainly Europeans who thought this way, for example, Jean Monnet and Robert Schuman. There were also influential Americans, members of the Department of State, whose view of the proper way to reconstitute Europe complemented those of key Europeans (Hogan 1984).

Still, the forces working in favor of nationalism and the nation-state were, and continue to be, formidable. An atmosphere of mutual distrust persisted, especially between France and Germany. Why would one expect this distrust to disappear in the aftermath of World War II? The French lobbied for detachment of the Ruhr from Germany and for reparations to be used to modernize the French economy (Hogan 1984, 2). The quest for reparations, along with increasing bilateralism in European relations, set the background for the Marshall Plan. The Marshall Plan (1947) was a large-scale effort launched by the United States to aid Europe in its economic and political recovery. By insisting that European states accept the aid on a multilateral basis, the Marshall Plan helped to establish the foundations for future intra-European cooperation.

A number of factors came together to support a multilateral effort to aid in Europe's recovery. First, the United States had a strong interest in putting Europe back on its feet collectively. In the minds of some officials in the U.S. State Department, there was no other way. With the collapse of the balance of power system and the emergence of the Soviet Union as a major power, the United States wanted to see a strong and united Western Europe. Economic integration was seen as a prerequisite for successful European action in other areas, political and military. Second, the United States realized that the European states were not likely to play their traditional balancing role globally. Thus, the United States faced power vacuums in the Balkans, the Middle East, and in Africa. The difficulties that Great Britain was having carrying out its responsibilities in Greece in 1946–1947 prompted the United States to develop its own Cold War foreign policy.

This chapter is organized around three dilemmas in the external relations of the EU. The first dilemma concerns the exclusive or non-exclusive nature of Europe's external relations. The EU has been charged with being "fortress Europe" at the same time that it is seen as a stepping stone to wider forms of cooperation. The former image conjures up a protectionist, inward-looking Europe concerned more with its own material satisfaction than with reaching out to the rest of the world. The latter image sees Europe as a pacific league of liberal states with extensive ties to Asia, Latin America, North Africa, and North America, anxious to build on its regional successes to further cooperation elsewhere. The second dilemma concerns the supposed trade-off between "widening" (expanding to new members) and "deepening" (increasing integration among existing members). This dilemma identifies a particularly timely debate since the EU is now actively considering applications from numerous states in Eastern and Central Europe. Many analysts and politicians fear that should the EU expand too far, it would become unwieldy, and threaten the efficiency of its political institutions. Others see a more complementary relationship between the two. The third dilemma concerns the ongoing construction of a Common Foreign and Security Policy (CFSP) in the EU. Here the focus is on the trade-off between creating a common foreign policy, and thus presumably having greater collective impact, versus each country going its individual way and retaining autonomy. In an environment of intense interdependence, states will have to choose between less effective policies that preserve sovereignty and common policies that sacrifice it.

FORTRESS EUROPE OR COSMOPOLITAN FORCE?

The postwar movement toward regional integration in Western Europe did not question the positive value of integration. The nation-state had suffered its second disastrous collapse in twenty-five years. Millions of lives had been lost and the economies and social structures of European countries lay in ruins. The European unity movement took shape in this atmosphere of defeat. European integration involved a search for something that was superior, including morally superior, to the exclusive organization of the world into territorial states. Through integration, Europeans could submerge their individual national identities in a joint endeavor. And by pooling its resources, Europe could hope to recover some of its lost political and economic strength.

However, for those on the outside, the formation of the European Economic Community (EEC) in the late 1950s was not unproblematic. The strongest opposition came from the Soviet Union and the countries of Eastern Europe who were joined with it in military and economic organizations (the Warsaw Treaty Organization ["Warsaw Pact"] and the Council for Mutual Economic Assistance [CMEA, or "Comecon"]). Soviet opposition was understandable. Creation of the EEC was seen to be part of the overall division of Europe into East and West, with the EEC emerging as the economic counterpart to the North Atlantic Treaty Organization (NATO). But fears and opposition were not limited to the Soviet Union. Doubts about the effects of the EEC and fears of exclusion and discriminatory treatment were evident in many parts of the world, not least in those European countries that were not original signatory members.

What were these fears? They ranged from the extreme, almost paranoid fear that Europe would become a world state, duplicating the problems of states on a much larger scale, to practical concerns about trade discrimination and the price of food in supermarkets. Specific fears were an expression of a more general concern that Western Europe would turn inward and become a provincial outpost, setting up economic barriers that benefited insiders and penalized outsiders.

While many of these fears were exaggerated, they did have a basis in social, economic, and political life in Western Europe. That is to say, an insular Europe, premised on Western Europe as a special entity, with its own civilization and economy, was not too far-fetched. Theologians like to think of Western Europe as the center of Christendom, the papacy, and the Holy Roman Empire. This idea of Europe as a cultural entity has some resonance in political science also. For example, Samuel Huntington argues that "The European Community rests on shared foundations of European culture and Western Christianity" (Huntington 1993). Economically, a region is never quite as good as the globe, in the sense that a larger, more comprehensive division of labor is more efficient than a smaller one. However, an economically integrated Europe of six countries would be large enough to capture regional gains from trade, encourage cross-border mergers among firms across borders, force the competitive restructuring of industries, and raise the level of real wealth. Politically, a unified Europe would increase the chances of survival of the types of political structures that have thrived in Europe, namely constitutional democracies, pluralistic interest group structures, and a mix of state planning and markets to guide allocation decisions in the economy. Also, on the less noble side of European goals, the EEC offered the opportunity to protect some of Europe's globally inefficient industries, as well as agriculture, and to seal Europe off from some of the "outside world's" trouble spots.

The opposite of Fortress Europe is cosmopolitan Europe. Europe is now imagined to be open, flexible, constantly reaching out to its global neighbors, playing a responsible global role, and serving as a cutting edge for a deeper, more efficient international division of labor. The political elite promoting a global Europe would be persons of broad, cosmopolitan

TABLE 4.1   Enlargements over Time

• Big Three, Small Three:	France, Italy, Germany, Belgium, Netherlands, Luxembourg (1958)
• Northern Three:	Denmark, Ireland, United Kingdom (1973)
• Southern Three:	Greece (1981), Spain and Portugal (1986)
• "New" Three:	Austria, Finland, Sweden (1995)

principles and humanistic training. The economic sectors behind a global Europe would be capital intensive and knowledge intensive. These sectors would profit from a global profile and would serve as the key constituencies for outward-oriented governing coalitions.

Regionalism is neither inherently provincial nor cosmopolitan. Stated in terms this broad, the question cannot be answered. Instead, I provide three more manageable foci around which to assess the evidence. These three foci have to do with commercial policy relationships between the integrating member states and the outside world, actual trade performance of Europe with the world, and the interaction between Europe as a region and global institutions in trade policy.

Commercial Policy Relations

The commercial policy of the EU has to do with its trade practices with non-member countries. A closed commercial policy would be one in which the EU tries to divert most of its trade activity inward, toward other members, and by implication away from non-members. Closure also implies fixed membership. To the extent that a customs union makes sense, it must have non-members, since the economic stimulus of the customs union comes from the difference between the internal and external barriers to trade. Thus, if the EU is closed and a "fortress Europe," we would expect few attempts at liberalization of trade relations with others.

What we observe is quite the contrary. The EU has both expanded to allow other countries to join and has trade ties with most countries in the world. The EU has absorbed (taken in as full members) nine countries that were not initial signatories (see Table 4.1). It has also associated itself with seventy ACP (African, Caribbean, and Pacific) states in the framework of the Lomé Conventions (Box 4.1) and created the European Economic Area (EEA) closely linking it to most non-EU Western European countries (see Box 4.2). Furthermore, it has developed a Mediterranean program from North Africa to the Middle East and has signed selective agreements with numerous Latin American and Asian countries. Finally, the EU is considering the applications of several countries of Central and Eastern Europe with a view to full membership (Bulgaria, the Czech Republic, Estonia,

Box 4.1   The Lomé Conventions

With four of its six original members as former colonial powers, the EU sought early on to develop close links with selected less developed countries (LDCs). Following from the
Yaoundé Conventions of 1963 and 1969, four Conventions
signed at Lomé, Togo (1975, 1979, 1984, and 1989), have
sought progressively to strengthen economic and political ties
between the EU and the countries of Africa, the Caribbean,
and the Pacific (ACP). These partner countries, which currently number seventy, benefit from unhindered access to the
EU's vast market, without having to offer reciprocal conces-
sions of their own. The Conventions have progressively moved
beyond simple trade and aid and increasingly include social,
environmental, and more overtly political provisions. Negotiations on Lomé V began in 1998. The end of the Cold War, domestic economic difficulties in the EU, and economic globalization have led the EU to call for a fundamental overhaul of
the Lomé framework during the 2000–2005 period.

Hungary, Latvia, Lithuania, Poland, Romania, Slovakia, and Slovenia). The
EU has either signed special agreements—known as Europe Agreements—
or has begun accession negotiations with these countries.

Since January 1, 1995, the European Union has been composed of fifteen member states (Austria, Finland, and Sweden were the latest members to join). The population of the EU is about 380 million people, making it larger than the United States whose population is about 270 million.
The combined gross domestic product (GDP) of the EU is very large. In
1997 it stood at 7,078 billion ECUs (European currency units), compared
to 6,062 ECUs for the US (*Eurostat: Facts and Figures* 1997). The EU accounts for 19.4 percent of world exports and 18.5 percent of imports, compared to 16.3 percent and 20.5 percent for the United States. Although a
great deal of the trade of the member states takes place within the region
(that is, among the members of the EU), trade ties to the "outside" world
are still extensive.

Thus, it is difficult to argue that the European Union is insular and inward-looking in terms of its commercial relationships with other countries. It has expanded from six to fifteen members and is likely to take in

Box 4.2 The European Economic Area (EEA)

On January 1, 1994, the EU and the member states of the European Free Trade Association (EFTA) created the European Economic Area (EEA). The EEA creates a vast single market ensuring the "four freedoms"—free movement of goods, services, capital, and labor—across almost all of Western Europe. The EFTA was initially created in 1959 as an alternative to the EEC for states that mistrusted supranationality (for example, the U.K. and Denmark) or sought to keep their distance from the West for fear of antagonizing the USSR (for example, Finland, Austria). Successive EU enlargements have reduced EFTA membership to four relatively small states: Iceland, Liechtenstein, Norway, and Switzerland. The Swiss rejected EEA membership in a 1992 referendum. The other three states now enjoy tight economic links with the EU, and although they have no political rights in the EU, they face the responsibility of adopting much of the *acquis communautaire* (see Box 4.3) into their domestic legislation. Given this and given changing political and economic circumstances in Europe, one might ask whether EFTA can survive and whether the EEA is a lasting structure or a halfway house on the road to full EU membership.

at least another ten member states in the coming decade. The EU is no longer simply Western Europe. Spain and Portugal are as much Southern as Western Europe, and Denmark, Finland and Sweden as much Northern Europe as Western. The next ten years will likely see increased representation from Central and Eastern Europe (Poland, Hungary, Slovenia, the Czech Republic) and the Baltics (Estonia, Latvia, and Lithuania). Indeed, Europe's openness would seem to be so apparent that the opposite specter of a large, all-encompassing Europe presents a more immediate worry. Even during the early seventies, Ralf Dahrendorf stated

> Sometimes the picture is drawn of a European Community which, along with the countries linked to it under preferential arrangements, already has a majority in GATT and which, after the entry of Britain, Denmark, Ireland, and Norway, is heading for a majority in the United Nations. There would be ten members, six remaining EFTA countries with still unclear links with the

Community, eighteen African states associated under the Yaoundé Agreement, and three under the Arusha Agreement, plus at least eight English-speaking countries in Africa after the entry of Britain, currently seven, and soon maybe thirteen, Mediterranean countries with preferential agreements—making a total of fifty-eight states already. Are we faced here with the emergence of an almost coherent regional bloc from the Arctic Circle to the northern frontier of South Africa? (Dahrendorf 1971, 149–150).

Trade Performance Data

The case for examining actual trade performance lies in the following observation. It is quite possible for the EU to be inclusive and generous in terms of its trade agreements toward nonmembers, and at the same time to alter its actual trade behavior toward them very little. Trade agreements are not ends in themselves. They are negotiated and signed in order to affect trade patterns among countries. However, trade agreements do not automatically change the import and export orientation of firms.

A number of factors affect trade, most importantly economic fundamentals such as productivity, consumer preferences, and comparative advantage. But precisely what do we look at when we look at trade performance? One indicator of regional openness-closure is the proportion of trade that is within the region to the amount of trade between regions. Figure 4.1 illustrates changes over time in exactly this indicator. The figure clearly shows that the percentage of within-region trade has increased within Europe (as it has within most other regions). Indeed, it has grown rather steadily and rather dramatically, so that whereas in 1970 intra-EC exports accounted for 50 percent of total exports, by 1995 this figure was over 62 percent. Almost two out of every three dollars (or Euros) of exports now has its origin and destination within the regional unit.

Increased levels of trade activity within the region, compared to between regions, may reflect an altered policy preference in favor of within-region partners. But it may not. It may simply be a function of underlying economic factors such as proximity, the changing volume of trade within the region, and shifting comparative advantages. Also, when tariffs are lowered and eliminated within the region but maintained against nonregional members, there is a shift in relative prices, which changes the relative incentives for doing business in favor of members. This is of course exactly what happens when internal tariffs are eliminated and external tariffs (the customs union part of the EU) are kept in place. In addition, trade is not necessarily zero-sum. That is, an increase of trade within the region does not necessarily imply a decrease of trade between that region and the rest of the world, as illustrated in Figure 4.2. Only if one starts with a fixed amount of trade would that be true. But trade may both re-

FIGURE 4.1   Intra-Regional Trade, 1970–1995

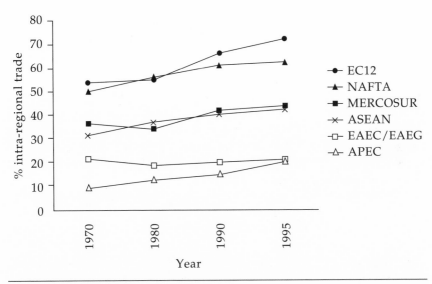

SOURCE: Grieco (1994, 40) for 1970–1990; IMF, *Direction of Trade Statistics Yearbook* (1996) for 1995.
NOTES: EC12 = France, Italy, Germany, Belgium, Netherlands, Luxembourg, Spain, Portugal, Greece, Denmark, Ireland, and the United Kingdom (assumes constant membership of twelve throughout the period); NAFTA = United States, Mexico, and Canada; MERCOSUR = Argentina, Brazil, Paraguay, and Uruguay; ASEAN = Brunei, Indonesia, Malaysia, Philippines, Singapore, and Thailand; EAEC/EAEG = ASEAN members and Japan, Hong Kong, South Korea, Taiwan, and perhaps Australia and New Zealand; APEC = ASEAN members, and United States, Canada, Australia, New Zealand, China, Taiwan, and Hong Kong.

flect increased domestic growth as well as stimulate further growth. In both cases, an increase of within-region trade may very well go hand in hand with increases of trade between regions.

An additional way in which trade-performance can be assessed is based on a theoretical analysis of expected trade relationships among members of a regional union and nonmembers. Economists evaluate their subject matter not only in terms of observed behavior, but also in terms of the kinds of predictions derived from their models. The theoretical arguments for and against a customs union are generally made in terms of its expected trade-creating versus trade-diverting aspects. Trade-creation occurs

when, as a result of the removal of trade barriers within a customs union, a member country replaces its own high-cost (formerly protected) production

FIGURE 4.2   Intra- and Extra-EU Trade, 1960–1996

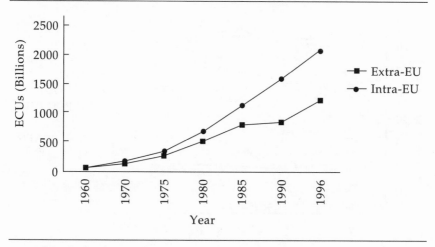

NOTE: Nominal values.
SOURCE: Eurostat, *External and Intra-European Union Trade: Statistical Yearbook,*
1958–1996 (Luxembourg: Office for Official Publications of the European Communities, 1997), pp. 11, 12, 21.

by imports from another member of the union. Trade diversion occurs when,
as a result of the removal of trade barriers within a customs union, a member
country replaces its imports from a low-cost non-union source, by a higher-
cost source within the union. The shift is caused by the newly created tariff
discrimination favoring union members (Viner 1950, 4).

In *The Customs Union Issue* (1950), Viner argued that the welfare impact
of a customs union should be assessed in terms of the differential between trade creation and trade diversion. The greater the trade creation
and the less the diversion of trade, the more beneficial the customs union.
The question now becomes one of determining which kinds of customs
unions are likely to produce varying levels of trade diversion and new
trade. Although this is a complicated issue, economists offer the following guidelines. A customs union is likely to have a beneficial impact to the
extent that (1) the economic area covered by the customs union is large;
(2) the average tariff levels on imports coming from countries outside the
customs zone are low compared to the tariff levels that would exist in the
absence of the union; and (3) there is a large differential in unit costs for
protected industries of the same kind in different areas within the customs union (Kreinin 1960, 372).

Although providing quantitative estimates of trade-diversion and
trade-creation can be very difficult, assessments have been made that can

tell us something. Before the EEC came into existence in 1958, a great deal of trade had already occurred among the six original members. The high level of within-region trade cut down on the potential for trade diversion. Also, tariffs toward nonmember countries were low from the beginning, and certainly not higher than the average of the tariff walls that member states had previously in place. After successive rounds of tariff negotiations under the General Agreement on Tariffs and Trade (GATT), external tariffs were lowered even further. Finally, while costs of production of similar goods within Europe are more similar today, there is good reason to believe that unit costs differed greatly from country to country when the EEC came into existence (1958). In this kind of international environment, tariff decreases would be expected to lead to large increases in trade volume and large gains from trade through elimination of inefficient industries (Kreinin 1960).

Regionalism and Globalism

The international economic order depends on openness. This is the essential principle underlying the international economic system since World War II, including the International Monetary Fund (IMF), the General Agreement on Tariffs and Trade, and the GATT's successor organization, the World Trade Organization (WTO). Yet regional organizations exist in many places around the globe and, indeed, at least twenty-five such regional organizations have been reported to the GATT since 1985.

Regions present an awkward problem from the standpoint of the global principles for organizing the world economy. They represent more openness than a world of autonomous nation-states. After all, regional unions represent groups of countries that are cooperating to reduce barriers to economic exchange. On the other hand, regions are preferential trade arrangements. They provide benefits to members and discriminate against nonmembers. The EU is a good example of such discrimination since members have zero tariffs against one another but a common tariff wall for nonmembers. As a result, these preferential trade areas (PTAs) distort trade patterns from what they would be in the absence of barriers, or even with constant barriers for all countries.

There are a number of ways to respond to regional organizations in general and the EU in particular. First of all, both the GATT and the United Nations (UN) have accepted regional organizations. The UN has rather elaborate rules for governing the relationship between regional and universal organizations. The GATT recognizes the legitimacy of regional organizations if such organizations conform to the requirements about average tariffs (they cannot be higher than before the union was formed) and trade-creation versus trade-diversion. As a result, many have accepted the EU as a second-best solution, given that the first-best solution (global free trade) is unattainable. In order to avoid allowing the best to be the enemy of the good, regional integration is defended as a useful approximation to global cooperation. The EU at least has free trade among the fifteen member states, and if free trade is desirable globally, it is also desirable regionally. Even if the EU does not serve as a springboard for more comprehensive global integration, it already has achieved a portion of what more comprehensive efforts are trying to achieve. Thus, the EU, North American Free Trade Agreement (NAFTA), the Southern Common Market (MERCOSUR), and the Association of Southeast Asian Nations (ASEAN) can all be defended on this "half a loaf" principle.

Not so, say critics of regional associations. As Jagdish Bhagwati has noted, regional associations are often presented as free trade areas when they are in fact preferential trade areas (PTAs). Bhagwati counts eighteen PTAs between the EU and other countries (Bhagwati 1997, 22). He adds two points to the traditional criticism of regional unions. The first point is that the discrimination offered by regional associations may be bad for member states too. It is not necessarily true that the benefits are captured internally and the costs externalized. If differential tariffs shift imports from nonmembers to members, it is the members themselves who bear the costs. Second, the half a loaf argument is utterly fallacious, critics say, in that defenders assume a direct relationship between reduction in tariff barriers and the corresponding level of protection. But, again relying on Bhagwati, a non-uniform reduction in tariffs can actually increase the total amount of protection (1997, 23).

The regional-global dilemma will never be fully resolved because the welfare effects of regionalism depend on factors that cannot be fully specified in advance. In particular, it is nearly impossible to know in advance whether a regional union will create more trade than it will divert. It is even more difficult to know whether a region sprouting up in Western Europe or Asia will merge with other associations or remain limited to original members.

There is one area where evidence has been accumulating about the relationship between the EU and global organizations and that has to do with trade relations in the GATT. As Kahler (1995) has argued, regionalism has been used as a bargaining tool within the GATT's Uruguay Round of tariff negotiations. In particular, U.S. President Clinton used the APEC (Asia Pacific Economic Cooperation) as a bargaining chip in the final stages of these negotiations, largely as a way of getting some leverage over the EU to reduce agricultural subsidies. Clinton elevated the APEC process just at the time when negotiations were stalled, and suggested that the United States would play the Asian hand if progress were not forthcoming in Europe. This no doubt stimulated reductions in protection on the part of the EU and paved the way toward a more comprehensive settlement in the Uruguay Round.

The overall relation between integration in the EU and the rest of the world is complex. However, certain patterns do emerge. Trade with non-member countries has flourished. It is impossible to know how fast trade would have grown in the absence of the EU. The only real-world comparison we have is trade with members before the EU formed compared with trade with those members after 1958. In this comparison, nonmember countries have done well. Economic theory about customs unions provides a series of yardsticks—most famously, trade-creation versus trade-diversion—that suggest that the EU has been beneficial. Finally, the EU has been very open in terms of accepting new members. The best proof of this is simply the expansion of its membership from six to fifteen. This, of course, poses its own dilemmas.

WIDENING VERSUS DEEPENING

One of the long-lasting debates about the EU concerns whether it should strive to be broad (including as many members as possible) or deep (characterized by authoritative and demanding political institutions as well as detailed policies across many issue areas). The British desire to make the EU (and previously the EEC) into a broad but politically weak free trade area symbolizes the broadening dimension whereas the German attempt to link monetary unification to strengthened political institutions symbolizes the other end of the continuum. Why should these two goals define a dilemma? The answer to this question is generally that as any community broadens, it takes in new members, and dilutes the community *esprit* somewhat. Presumably the members with the greatest enthusiasm will come on board first, followed by those with lesser appreciation for the common institution. So as additional members are added, there is a diminishing marginal enthusiasm (or loyalty), with the net result that average loyalty decreases.

In addition, more members mean that there is a greater opportunity for casting the veto. When qualified majority voting (QMV) is not the rule, and unanimity is required, each member can cast a veto unilaterally and block progress. Thus the number of blocking points increases in direct proportion to the number of voting members. As more and more members are added, it is likely that heterogeneity (defined in terms of disparate positions) will go up. This need not be the case. It could happen that new members are just as likely to vote with the majority as older members are, but this would not be the most likely outcome. Those who are most cohesive are likely to join the organization first. Britain, Ireland, and Denmark, who joined in 1973, all had different interests compared with the original six members, and many of those differences persisted after membership.

Finally, even if cohesion does not weaken with the addition of new members, collective action problems will increase. A collective action problem occurs when actors (in this case countries) want the same outcome but there are incentives for some (or all) not to work toward these outcomes. Perhaps the benefits will be non-excludable, as in the case of clean air, a better regulatory environment, collective defense, or some policy that preserves common property resources. When this is the case, countries will have incentives to free-ride on the public benefits provided by others.

Short of such free-riding, we can note that the notion of a small subset of states, a core, will be much less persuasive in a larger group. France and Germany could easily lead the way in a Community of Six. With each enlargement of the EU, however, their potential for influence has steadily declined, as has that of all members (see Hosli 1993 and Kerremans 1998 for helpful discussions). As illustrated in Table 4.2, Germany and France each used to have 33 percent of the required minimum number of votes needed to pass legislation (the "qualified majority"), although they enjoy less than half that in today's fifteen member EU. The fraction of votes needed to pass legislation has risen steadily, whereas (by extension) the number able to block it has steadily dropped. The greater the number of actors, the harder it will be to coordinate actions.

For the first several decades of the Community's history, the Franco-German alliance served as the crucial core of a pro-integration coalition. If France and Germany could agree on the need for cooperation on a particular issue, such as liberalization of trade or a common agricultural policy, progress was very likely. Similarly, during the mid-eighties, agreement among Germany, the United Kingdom, and France was crucial to progress on the single market and the signing of the Single European Act (SEA). As new members are added, and particularly as the Community contemplates expansion into Eastern and Central Europe, the importance of the Franco-German alliance (an alliance within an alliance) diminishes. Thus the special relationships nurtured by Charles de Gaulle and Konrad Adenauer, by Giscard d'Estaing and Helmut Schmidt, and by Francois Mitterrand and Helmut Kohl, which resulted in the important moves forward in the integration process, no longer seem as crucial as they once did.

While it is neither a fact of logic nor a force of nature that wider means less deep, there are certainly a lot of factors that work in that direction. However, for a variety of reasons to be explored below, expansion to widen the EU has not generally been at the cost of depth to either the institutions of the EU or the functional scope of the integration process.

TABLE 4.2   Votes in the Council of Ministers

	EC6	EC9	EC10	EC12	EC15
Belgium	2	5	5	5	5
	16.67%	12.20%	11.11%	9.26%	8.06%
Netherlands	2	5	5	5	5
	16.67%	12.20%	11.11%	9.26%	8.06%
Luxembourg	1	2	2	2	2
	8.33%	4.88%	4.44%	3.70%	3.23%
Italy	4	10	10	10	10
	33.33%	24.39%	22.22%	18.52%	16.13%
France	4	10	10	10	10
	33.33%	24.39%	22.22%	18.52%	16.13%
Germany	4	10	10	10	10
	33.33%	24.39%	22.22%	18.52%	16.13%
Denmark		3	3	3	3
		7.32%	6.67%	5.56%	4.84%
Ireland		3	3	3	3
		7.32%	6.67%	5.56%	4.84%
United Kingdom		10	10	10	10
		24.39%	22.22%	18.52%	16.13%
Greece			5	5	5
			11.11%	9.26%	8.06%
Spain				8	8
				14.81%	12.90%
Portugal				5	5
				9.26%	8.06%
Austria					4
					6.45%
Finland					3
					4.84%
Sweden					4
					6.45%
Qualified Majority[a]	12	41	45	54	62
	70.59%	70.69%	71.43%	71.05%	71.26%
Blocking Minority[a]	6	18	19	23	26
	35.29%	31.03%	30.16%	30.26%	29.89%
Total Votes	17	58	63	76	87

Top figure in each cell is the number of votes. Bottom figure is number of votes as percentage of the qualified majority.
[a] As percentage of total votes.

Expansion from Original Six to Nine Members

In 1973, the European Community took on three new members: the United Kingdom, Denmark, and Ireland. Two of these three countries (the United Kingdom and Denmark), former members of the European Free Trade Association (EFTA), were reluctant partners. While they desired the benefits of free trade and international specialization, they were not advocates of deep integration. Indeed, in the late 1950s the United Kingdom spearheaded the plan for creating the EFTA as a looser alternative to the EEC, an association that was to provide all the benefits of economic association while not compromising the sovereignty and autonomy of the member states. Their application for membership in the European Community signaled the fact that their economies had become more closely tied to those of the Six with the result that the coordination of their policies with the Six became imperative.

Membership of the United Kingdom, Denmark, and Ireland was not expected to speed up the deepening of integration in the Community. To be fair, the Community had already stagnated, at least economically. Since the Luxembourg Compromise in early 1966 (see Chapter 3, Box 3.2), the Community had been operating under the veto system. One could hardly expect the membership of these three EFTA countries to make things worse in an institutional sense.

Institutional deepening was taking place during the same period that membership expanded. The Chapter on social policy discussed the revolutionary doctrines that the Court of Justice laid down regarding the direct effect of the Treaty and Regulations. During the seventies and early eighties, the ECJ expanded the doctrine of direct effect to cover Directives, a different class of Community legislation, in the *Van Duyn* case (Case 41/74, [1974] ECR 1337). As a result, the idea of direct effect was not limited to the language of the Treaty of Rome, but also applied to certain kinds of secondary legislation.

The institutional deepening fostered by the Court's jurisprudence was not limited to bestowing rights on individuals. The Court also took the lead in terms of placing the powers and responsibilities of the different institutions of the Community on a firm basis. In the *Isoglucose* cases (Cases 138 and 139/79, [1980] ECR 3337, 3393), the ECJ confirmed an important principle of separation of powers when it held that the Council of Ministers must consult the Parliament before it legislates. The Parliament had not yet delivered its opinion when the Council adopted a proposal set before it by the Commission. The Court annulled this legislative act, saying that a fundamental principle of democracy is that the people shall take part in the exercise of power through its representative institutions (Mancini and Keeling 1994, 178; Kirchner and Williams 1983). The Court helped to establish an important foundation of democratic institutions—the separation of powers—and it enhanced the standing of the European Parliament by requiring that it be consulted by the Council. The Court has continued this line of reasoning, with nuances, in a string of cases through to the present day.

It is true that the deepening of institutions through the actions of the Court does not result from explicit bargains among states in either the European Council or Council of Ministers. For this reason, some would discount the importance of these events, as if the Court's jurisprudence could only be meaningful if it were set forth at the behest of the executives of the member states. The period from 1968 to 1985 is portrayed as a time when the Council of Ministers and Commission, the two organs most central to the passage of Community legislation, were able to accomplish very little. However, we should keep in mind that the European Council was formed in 1974 and the European Monetary System (EMS) was launched in 1979. Despite the failure of many initiatives of the Council and Commission, the Court's case law advanced political integration in the area of individual rights and the separation of powers, among others. Thus, there was an institutional deepening of the EU even during a period of expansion.

From Nine to Twelve and the SEA

In 1981 Greece became a member of the EC, and in 1986 Spain and Portugal joined, bringing membership in the Community to twelve. Expansion to twelve posed two distinct dangers. The first was that twelve members would simply be too unwieldy. The second was that the three newest members were from the South, that is, they were poorer members who would make demands on scarce Community resources. Because the newest three members increased the heterogeneity of membership, even more stagnation was expected. These were difficult times for the Community. Economically, the members were still suffering from two oil shocks of the 1970s. Many economies were not growing and at the same were experiencing inflation, two economic "bads" that did not traditionally come together. This gave rise to a new term, *stagflation*. In addition, since the important activities of the Court went generally unrecognized, most observers thought the Community itself was in an institutional deep-freeze since the Luxembourg Compromise.

Given the possibility that three new members might dilute the EC, it was important to have some initiative to keep the integration process going. The advances embodied in the Single European Act (1987) leading to the completion of the internal market by January of 1993 were very important. The SEA provided for the elimination of all barriers to the flow of goods, services, and productive factors across national borders by the end of 1992. The White Paper leading up to the SEA outlined almost 300 proposals identifying specific obstacles to free movement. The SEA not only promised to make Europe more efficient, but it also entailed a proposal for institutional changes, specifically, a movement away from the veto to majority voting for measures related to the internal market.

The United Kingdom was important in the decision to liberalize the internal market, and in a more modest way, Greece, Spain, and Portugal also played a role. It was the convergence of interests among the United Kingdom and Germany to deregulate the market that formed the crucial support for the 1992 program (Moravcsik 1991; Cameron 1992). France, ruled by the Socialist Party, went along, but it was hardly a Socialist project to lubricate the flow of capital and labor (mostly capital after all) across national lines. President Mitterrand agreed with the initiative because he had few options and because the crucial lessons for France had been learned already in 1983, when France had been disciplined by international capital markets. When the United Kingdom entered the Community, it might have been thought unlikely that a coalition between the UK and Germany would propel the Community forward. It would certainly have been thought unlikely if this forward movement were to include institutional changes in the direction of majority voting. Yet this is precisely what the SEA entailed.

Some observers thought that Greece, Spain, and Portugal would lose a lot by the liberalization of the market. After all, doesn't protection operate to shield weaker industries and services? Precisely the same can be said for factor rigidities, that is, restrictions on the flow of capital and labor, whether these restrictions stem from political regulations, custom, or organizational factors such as personal ties between producers, banks, and retail stores. One line of thought prevalent when the SEA came into existence was that the weaker economies would be swamped by Germany, France, and the United Kingdom.

The best economic studies available leading up to the SEA showed that the poorer countries would gain, and gain plenty, by liberalization (Marks 1992, 199). However, it is not clear from these studies what the public at large, never known for its appreciation of econometric analysis, thought. It is also likely that the very gains expected from liberalization would require extensive restructuring of industries in the poorer countries, although some of the gains were projected to materialize from increases in economies of scale within industries already in place. If such were the case, the downside risks of perfecting the market would have been considerable, and Southern support could not have been taken for granted. Yet, Spain, Greece, and Portugal went along with liberalization of the market and with the institutional proposal for QMV on market-related measures. It is of course true that these three countries were persuaded by the promise of increases in structural funds, much of which would go to poorer regions within Spain, Greece, and Portugal.

It is not difficult to see why the United Kingdom wanted to deregulate the European market. This corresponded to Thatcher's domestic program for privatization and deregulation. But why did Thatcher accept QMV? The Commission tied together two goals, one of which the UK wanted badly (deregulation) and one of which it did not want at all (QMV). Thatcher made her point at the Milan Summit in 1985, stating that QMV was an unnecessary institutional change. She argued that the frustration with economic stagnation, the continuing pressure of business interests, and the simple good sense of going ahead with completion of the market, were the best assurances that the market would be completed (Dinan 1999, 24). But Thatcher failed to convince her colleagues, and QMV became part of the SEA. In what may seem a quirk of fate, the UK, the most vociferous opponent of institutional deepening, went along with narrowing the range of the veto, a decision that had an impact on the voting rules adopted in the Maastricht and Amsterdam Treaties.

German Unification and Eastward Expansion

As suggested earlier, the Franco-German alliance has formed the core of the Community system. However, the Germany involved in that alliance was the Cold War Germany whose capital was Bonn, whose global ambitions were modest, and whose population was in the neighborhood of fifty-five million. By contrast, the Germany that existed after reunification in October 1990 was a much larger country of eighty million people and five additional *Länder* (roughly equivalent to provinces or states). The revolutionary process that began with the collapse of communism in the Soviet Union and Eastern Europe, the tearing down of the Berlin Wall, and the incorporation of the five *neue Länder* (new states) into the former Federal Republic of Germany altered the balance between France and Germany. French power rested on the performance of its economy, the skill and creativity of its diplomatic elite, and the absence of alternative partners for Germany within the EC. Among the original Six, Germany could not really choose to go it alone with Italy, or with Belgium, the Netherlands, or Luxembourg. While France surely needed Germany to move forward with any serious proposal, so too did Germany need France. Their best alternative to working with the other was so unattractive that the prospect of non-agreement stimulated progress. This was to change, asymmetrically, in Germany's favor.

A larger Germany tilting toward the East, with potential allies in the United Kingdom, Denmark, and the Benelux countries, made France less indispensable. Further, with the collapse of the Warsaw Pact and the Council of Mutual Economic Assistance (CMEA), it appeared to be a matter of time before countries from Central and Eastern Europe would apply for membership. What was unthinkable several years earlier, namely membership of Poland, Hungary, and Czechoslovakia (soon to be the Czech Republic and Slovakia) in the European Community, now seemed highly likely. Needless to say, this upset the delicate balance of power between France and Germany in favor of Germany. This change in power relations, itself a result of broadening to include the former East Germany, was to have consequences for the institutional deepening of the Community.

Oddly enough, it was an economic issue that was to provide the key opportunity to resolve the political problem of a *gross Deutschland* (a big Germany). With monetary unification on the agenda in 1990, the issue was what kind of monetary integration to support. Proposals ranged from the relatively weak suggestion to continue with coordinated exchange rates, even fixing them for periods of time, all the way to a common currency with a European Central Bank. The common currency clearly called for the highest sacrifices of national sovereignty and the deepest commitment to institutional integration. Despite the fact that exchange rate volatility could have been managed with a less demanding regime, it was the proposal for deep monetary integration that won the day. How do we account for this?

As discussion of monetary issues proceeded, the chief executives of the member states decided to call an Intergovernmental Conference (IGC) on political institutions that ran parallel to the one on monetary unification. The "imminence of German unification, the need for a Community *Ostpolitik* (a policy toward Eastern Europe), and the prospect of further enlargement made a compelling case for deeper integration" (Dinan 1998, 32). Once again, it was Kohl and Mitterrand, leaders of the Franco-German alliance, who got the ball rolling by sending a letter to the Council presidency in April 1990 stressing the need to move ahead on the political front.

Neither France nor Germany could press for deeper political institutionalization without reservations, but both also had compelling reasons to move forward. For France, political and economic institutions in the form of a common currency and a European Central Bank (ECB) would provide assurances that monetary policy would be decided around the table, according to a system of rules. It is true that Germany would have a big role in shaping these rules, and it is also true that the structure of the monetary institutions would look a lot like the parallel institutions inside Germany. But France was not bargaining from a position of strength. It was really in no position to dictate the details of monetary institutions to Germany, nor in the end to deny unification for Germany. For France, the most likely alternative to deeper monetary unification was a looser, more decentralized system of exchange-rate coordination in which the Mark and the franc would compete in international markets, with predictable consequences. Since the German economy is stronger, the franc would not be able to compete with the Mark, causing devaluation of the French currency. France would be less powerful than Germany both within a rule-based system and within less regulated international capital markets. But it would be relatively less disadvantaged operating within a system of rules.

On strictly economic grounds, it may seem that Germany had little to gain by European monetary integration, as embodied in EMU (Economic and Monetary Union). After all, Germany had done quite well under the less demanding European Monetary System (EMS). As Moravcsik points out, the EMS had contributed to the undervaluation of the Mark, which in turn made Germany's exports more competitive on global markets. And it did all this with little adverse effect on Germany's autonomy (Moravcsik 1998, 391). Thus it is hard to explain Germany's enthusiasm for EMU.

One reason that Germany supported EMU as established in the 1993 Maastricht Treaty is that German leadership simply wanted strong European institutions to bind themselves into Europe. It was partly an intrinsic question of German identity (are we European or an autonomous state free to play balance of power politics?) and partly a deft political move to placate Germany's European partners, who no doubt feared that a *gross Deutschland* could not easily fit into Europe as a whole. The enlarged Federal Republic of Germany had a border with Poland, the Cold War was now over, and Eastern Europe was no longer under the thumb of the former Soviet Union. Surely under these greatly altered circumstances Germany would tilt to the East, expand its economic and cultural ties, and recreate a zone of German influence in Central and Eastern Europe. Thus Kohl was keenly aware that it was good politics to bind Germany into Western institutions. Such a policy merely represented the continuation of Germany's historic two-step since World War II. Each time Germany acquired more of its sovereignty and autonomy, it was accompanied by some measure of increased integration into Western institutions. This can be seen with Germany's membership in the ECSC (shortly after the Federal Republic came into existence), with Germany joining NATO as it was granted increased autonomy in 1954, with the appearance of *Ostpolitik* just before European Political Cooperation (EPC) in 1969, and the latest tandem of reunification and monetary integration (Tewes 1998, 120).[1]

What is so interesting about the widening of the Community is that turbulence in the international environment associated with German reunification did not disrupt the internal workings of the EC, quite the opposite. Turbulence in international markets persuaded the French to accept institutional commitments they most assuredly would not have liked on ideological grounds. As Jean-Louis Bourlanges put it in an article in *Le Figaro* (June 26, 1995), "we (meaning the French) want a strong Europe, like the Germans, but with weak institutions, like the British" (Menon 1996, 239). Institutions were not pursued for intrinsic reasons, as an end in themselves, but simply to promote a concrete, economic goal.

The reunification of Germany led it in the same direction as France. Germany accepted EMU because it was the perfect institutional symbol to ease the fears of its European allies. Also, since the German business community and the *Bundesbank* played such an important role in setting conditions to EMU, Germany's economic interests were not expected to suffer. Upon unification, among Kohl's first public statements was that Germany wished for a "European Germany" and not a "German Europe." Such pronouncements might have been treated as pure rhetoric were it not for the fact that Germany committed itself to a binding form of institutional integration inside the EU. Finally, in January of 1995, Austria, Finland, and Sweden joined the EU. All these were previously neutral during the Cold War (1947–1990) period. As small, relatively wealthy countries, they did not present the same kinds of divisions that were soon to be raised by the new applicants from Central and Eastern Europe.

Future Expansion into Central and Eastern Europe and Deepening

The Cold War division of Europe was premised on the existence of two blocs, East and West. Between these two blocs almost all of Europe was carved up and assigned membership, except for a small group of neutrals who themselves had stern constraints on their actions. Austria, Sweden, Finland, and Yugoslavia may not have been members of the Western or Eastern blocs but they (perhaps except for Sweden) could not just choose to sign up for one side or the other. The Western bloc was led militarily by the NATO (with the United States at the helm) and the Eastern bloc by the Warsaw Treaty Organization (WTO), (with the Soviet Union leading). The EU was the economic arm of the West as the CMEA was the economic arm of the East. Membership was clear and did not shift, except for the addition of a few states, crossovers did not occur, and bloc-to-bloc interactions were minimal. There was very little trade, capital flows, technology transfer, migration, tourism, or legal transmission of information between East and West. Churchill's "iron curtain" metaphor was not literally true, but the boundary between East and West could not have worked much more effectively if it had been made of iron.

With the end of the Cold War, the geopolitical architecture of Europe came into immediate question. The Eastern pillar of the bipolar system collapsed, immediately calling into question the rationale for the Western pillar. Given the familiar clarity and symmetry of the bipolar world, the West felt a bit awkward with NATO, less so with the EC. In any case, the Soviet Union fell apart, giving way to nationalist pressures from its Republics. Soon there were fifteen sovereign states where previously there had been but one. At the same time, the Soviet's empire in Eastern Europe gave way. CMEA, with its planned and enforced international division of labor, so antithetical to the principles of capitalism, was disbanded, as was the Warsaw Pact. Certainly there was little grass-roots sentiment in favor of keeping either organization in existence.

The collapse of the Soviet Union and the Communist regimes in Eastern Europe opened up new possibilities. Europe could be organized as a system of independent states along pre–World War II lines, with each state judging according to changing circumstances which international posture was best. The major states of Europe could opt for a loose form of international concert in which the members attempted to coordinate their actions but accepted no common institutions and did not delegate sovereignty. Or European states could come together under one or several regional organizations such as the EU, the Organization for Security and Cooperation in Europe (OSCE), and the UN's Economic Commission for Europe (ECE).

An independent state system was seen as too dangerous, vulnerable to Russian revanchism, and likely to create uncertainty in an environment where too many things were already in flux. Neutrality made no sense. The structural conditions in terms of the distribution of power simply did not warrant neutrality (neutrality from what or in relationship to what?). Neutrality always presumed that there were major powers who opposed membership in one or the other bloc, and who were prepared to act to ensure continued neutrality. The only viable option was for the newly independent Central and Eastern European countries (CEECs) to seek EU membership.

This is of course exactly what happened. The CEECs applied for membership: Poland and Hungary in 1994; Slovakia, Romania, and Bulgaria in 1995; the Czech Republic in 1996. Soon, Slovenia, Estonia, Latvia, Lithuania, Cyprus, and Malta also applied. The EU was faced with a roster of countries anxious to acquire membership and willing to do their best to meet the stringent conditions set down by the EU as part of the accession strategy. It is conceivable that the EU could have twenty-five to twenty-seven members by the middle of the first decade of the new millennium. It is conceivable, although it is difficult to imagine what the day-to-day operation of the EU would look like. For example, how would the Council of Ministers, with a representative from each state, operate? Would it be possible to accomplish anything? Such a Council would look more like the upper house of a national legislature (the German *Bundesrat* for example) than a small cartel of national executives.

The potential trade-off between widening and deepening was thought of from the start. The EU did not simply rush into eastward expansion and then try to figure out what it all meant for its institutions. There were three phases through which applicant countries moved. The first phase was marked by aid from the EU to the applicants. This phase was aimed not only at economic and social restructuring but also at the nurturing of civil society, democratic institutions, civic education, respect for minorities, and human rights. The Poland-Hungary Actions for Economic Reconstruction (PHARE) program, aimed first at Poland and Hungary, was generalized to other countries. The commitment to building the institutions of civil society was always high. The aim was never just to pour money into these countries with the belief that capitalism, and capitalist democracy, would spring up naturally (Dimitrova 1998, 321).

The second phase was marked by "Europe Agreements." These Agreements recognized that the applicants who signed them were intent on becoming EU members, and it was their purpose to prepare countries for precisely this eventuality (Piening 1997, 58; Dimitrova 1998, 325). Poland, Hungary, and Czechoslovakia negotiated agreements in 1991. The Polish and Hungarian accords came into operation in 1994 followed a year later by similar measures in Bulgaria and Romania. The Agreements undertook specific steps to bring about economic reforms with an eye toward membership and political reforms that would satisfy the democratic requirements of the EU. Accession to the EU implied that applicant countries were stable democracies, had functioning market economies which could withstand competitive pressures, and were willing to accept the daunting *acquis communautaire* (see Box 4.3). Becoming a member was a serious business, from both ends of the negotiating table. Allowing members in who were neither democratic nor capitalist would pose insuperable problems for those already in. Past achievements could easily unravel. For applicant states, future membership was conditional on difficult restructuring: privatization, replacement of the plan by the market mechanism, establishment of private property rights, respect for contracts (which implied contract law and courts), tolerance and respect for the rights of others, political competition, retraining programs for the police, and guidance for lawyers concerning individual rights.

The third phase was ushered in by the Copenhagen Summit in June of 1993, at which the European Council gave its full stamp of approval to future membership on the part of signatories to the Europe Agreements. Five years after this Summit, five of the signatories to these Agreements were proceeding with accession negotiations (Serfaty 1999, 47). Poland, Hungary, the Czech Republic, Estonia, and Slovenia were included in this first wave. Others were to follow later.

Box 4.3   The *Acquis Communautaire*

The *acquis communautaire* refers to everything that the EU has achieved since its early origins in the European Coal and Steel Community (ECSC). It comprises treaties, binding secondary legislation, court judgments and, more informally, the rules and norms of EU governance. For many years acceptance of the *acquis*, albeit often over significant transition periods, has been the *sine qua non* of adhesion to the EU by new members. However, the advent of "variable geometry," or a "multi-speed Europe," in which subsets of member states can move forward in given areas without their EU partners, may alter this conception of the *acquis* and may lead to new criteria for membership in the Union.

How would accession of new members affect the institutional structure of the EU? The potential trade-off between widening and deepening was never more pointed. This was due in part to the sheer number of countries expected to join. It was simply difficult to imagine how the Commission and Council of Ministers would operate with a representative from each country. Bart Kerremans (1998, 94–95) has calculated a measure of legislative control exercised by each member state under different assumptions about number of members and the minimum number of votes required to pass legislation. With just six member states (from 1958 to 1973), Germany, France, and Italy each had 33 percent of the qualified majority needed to pass legislation. In a Community of twenty-seven, ninety-four votes will be required to pass legislation under QMV, meaning that the share of Germany, France, and Italy drops to 10 percent each. Estonia, Latvia, and Lithuania will each control 2.1 percent, 3.1 percent, and 3.1 percent respectively. These small voting shares do not necessarily imply voting impotence, since it is possible that these votes could be pivotal (that is, crucial to a winning coalition) in a large number of cases. Looked at in another way, the smallest number of countries needed to meet the QMV threshold was three in a Community of six, nine in a Community of fifteen, and fourteen in a Community of twenty-seven. Even under the most favorable circumstances where the large member states are in agreement, fourteen countries must agree for legislation to pass (Kerremans 1998, 94–95).

Difficulties in Community decisionmaking may increase in two other ways. Diversity of membership will increase with influx of members from Central and Eastern Europe. Most of the prospective members are poor by EU standards. By way of comparison, the four poorest current member states have incomes about 75 percent of the EU average. But for the ten applicant countries, the mean income is barely one-third of the EU average (Serfaty 1999, 48). This could easily create a new North-South divide, with Spain, Greece, Portugal, and Ireland aligning with the newest member states in their search for more structural funds for the poorest regions. The Community has never been a distributive state; it has instead advanced through market-making, market-perfection (controlling externalities), and regulation. With a budget that is less than one and a half percent of the collective GDPs of the member states, it is easy to see how such a coalition would put a strain on Community resources.

I have already mentioned how France would be affected by such a move to the East. France's interests are extremely sensitive to the widening-deepening debate because Franco-German cohesion has been central to European integration. With Germany's move to the East, France will have to tolerate a *de facto* German sphere of influence in Central and Eastern Europe. These lands are Germany's natural turf. With strong economic and cultural ties to the old Austro-Hungarian Empire, Central Europe, and Eastern Europe, Germany's influence will increase. And if power in the end is not about military force but more about the relative ability to go one's own way, then clearly Germany will be hurt less than France, and France's influence will decline.

In addition, and perhaps most important of all, France has always attempted to combine effective policymaking with consensus, that is, with the search for unanimous agreement. In a smaller, more homogenous Community, this was possible. But in an enlarged Community that also increases diversity, this is less likely. As a result, France is likely to resort to an emphasis on the intergovernmental dimension of decisionmaking. France has already attempted to tie enlargement to reinforcement of the powers of the Council of Ministers. It has done so not by insisting on the veto, but by linking Council powers to a re-weighting of votes so as to better represent the position of the larger states (Menon 1996, 244–245). France is in the same position as it was in regard to EMU, with the weaker economic terrain and attempts to correct this loss by strengthening its position within the EU's institutions. But strengthening one's position in Community institutions is a tricky business. Emphasis on the veto is a two-edged sword. The veto implies an ability to obstruct, but if everyone has a veto, this means that nothing may get done when France wants something done. Thus, France is working more for a scheme of voting which gives it more voting power, while relying on the veto only to preserve important national values (Menon 1996, 244–245).

For Germany, movement to the East presents costs and benefits. On the one hand, eastward expansion seems inevitable, since to leave the CEECs out of the Community is to expose them to a resurgence of Russian power and nationalism. The more clearly the markers are thrown down, the more stable relations will be. Russian aggression (or Serbian, Ukrainian) against Poland and the Czech Republic may not be likely at all, but the probability is much lower with these countries incorporated within NATO and the EU. Then aggression would be very costly because the other member states would be likely to come to the aid of fellow member states.

Germany has been the historic defender of not sacrificing deepening in favor of widening in the EU. The reasons for this are clear. Germany's role in World War II has made it a pariah state for much of the post-war period. Germany's path to recognition and autonomy has been intimately bound up with membership in European institutions: NATO, ECSC, the EEC, the Council of Europe and the Organization for Security and Cooperation in Europe (OSCE). Thus, for Germany, the opportunity for eastward expansion clashed with its commitment to deep institutional integration in the EU. This conflict was "solved" by choosing both broadening and deepening. This was carried out by supporting membership for the CEECs but at the same time attaching conditions which were quite stringent, and which required the new members to demonstrate in costly ways their sincerity about joining. The CEECs were required to demonstrate movement to a market economy, the ability to withstand global competitive pressure, the stability of institutions guaranteeing democracy and human rights, and capacity and willingness to absorb the *acquis communautaire*, the vast corpus of legislation and procedures adopted by the earlier members (Dimitrova 1998, 327).

In short, Germany was able to overcome its *Mittellage* (middle condition) between Western and Eastern Europe by thoroughly binding its Eastern neighbors to its own West. It did this by assuring that the countries of Eastern Europe did not simply enhance ties to Germany but also became solid members of the European Union and the North Atlantic Treaty Organization. Only by doing this could Germany turn back criticism of its European neighbors that it was playing the East against the West. As the former East bloc countries moved toward membership in the EU and NATO, countries previously in the East became part of the West (Tewes 1998, 121).

Despite the will to enlarge eastward, the foregoing discussion suggests that the next enlargement poses serious institutional challenges to the EU. The Maastricht Treaty, originally agreed just weeks before the Christmas 1991 dissolution of the Soviet Union, had recognized that the prospect of

FIGURE 4.3   Council Representation, 1999

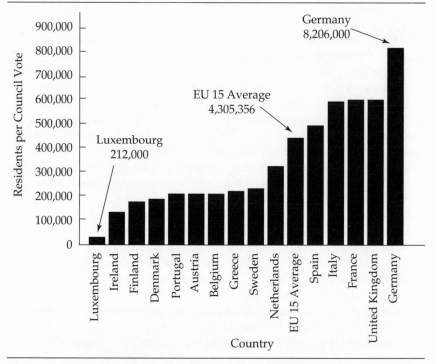

SOURCE: 1999 Population figures from Eurostat; author's calculations.

widening would require adaptations to the EU's central institutions. Member states and Community officials met during 1996–1997 in an Intergovernmental Conference (IGC) that culminated in the mid-1997 signing of the Amsterdam Treaty. This IGC had as its central purpose the rationalization of Community institutions to pave the way for enlargement, and although it succeeded in other areas, in this most critical area it failed dismally. Throughout the IGC, the expectation was that member states would craft a "package deal" in which larger states (France, Germany, the United Kingdom) would win a re-weighting of votes in the Council of Ministers in exchange for giving up one of their two European Commissioners. This would serve simultaneously to correct the egregious over-representation of the smaller states in the Council (see Figure 4.3) and rationalize the bloated European Commission, in which twenty commissioners chose a dozen or so meaningful policy portfolios. It would also settle the question of the voting weights to be assigned to the Eastern candidates for entry and of the new thresholds for qualified majorities and blocking minorities, which had created serious frictions in the run-up to the (easier) 1995 enlargement. The EU's inability to respond to this challenge suggests two things. First, yet another IGC, this one devoted largely or exclusively to enlargement and institutional issues, began in early 2000. Second, despite synergies in the past, deepening and widening represent an ongoing dilemma of European integration.

COMMON FOREIGN AND SECURITY POLICY (CFSP) VERSUS SEPARATE NATIONAL INTERESTS

Henry Kissinger, when he was secretary of state during the 1970s, posed an interesting question: "If I want to call Europe" he asked, "what phone number do I use?" (Cheysson 1997, 35). The question is interesting because it has no obvious answer and because Europe, even the EU, does not speak with one voice in foreign policy. In international politics, we take it for granted that countries are represented by single leaders who speak on behalf of their constituencies. It is difficult to negotiate with a country that has no clear leader. Without clear lines of authority, enforcement of agreements would be uncertain at best. But within the EU it is precisely this assumption of a unitary actor that is questioned. Kissinger put his finger on a particularly important issue. His question, while perhaps provocative, concisely summed up the difficulties of finding a coherent European voice in foreign policy.

Short of producing a single phone number, we can at least ask where the sources of foreign policymaking lie within Europe. There are the individual states, each of which has an executive and a ministry of foreign affairs. States have been, and to a large extent still are, the sites where foreign policy, particularly the military security aspect of foreign policy, is made. In addition, there is the North Atlantic Treaty Organization (NATO), composed of nineteen members today, which coordinates foreign policy for the North Atlantic world, and which has played a large role in the various wars in Yugoslavia. Presumably, the Europe of which Kissinger spoke is the EU, but even here the picture is very cloudy. Should Kissinger look for the phone number in the Council of Ministers (specifically the Ministers of Foreign Affairs), the European Council of Heads of States, or the European Commission's Directorate General dealing with External Relations, and which one (there are several)? The new Commission named by Romano Prodi, in July of 1999, has no less than four people "in charge" of various aspects of foreign policy. Chris Patten is in charge of Foreign Relations, Pascal Lamy has responsibility for foreign trade, Gunter Verheugen deals with the thorny enlargement issues, and Poul Nielson heads the section dealing with relations between the EU and the Third World. In addition, at the beginning of 2000, Javier Solana, formerly secretary general of NATO, took over the new job of High Representative within the Council of Ministers ("Mr. CFSP") and is responsible for coordinating Common Foreign and Security Policy. It is not unusual for governments to divide responsibilities for various aspects of external relations, particularly when they include economic and security relations. But the various portfolios within the EU Commission (and Solana's outside the Commission) are not always clear of their charges; indeed, they seem to be purposively blurred. In an age when the EU is thinking about improving transparency and accountability, the institutional arrangements for foreign policy are confused.

The main dilemma posed by CFSP has to do with states acting on the basis of national interest or acting to promote a common foreign policy. If each state pursues its own objectives with its own means, it may have little impact, particularly in a world of interdependence. Just imagine individual countries in the EU pursuing their own monetary policy or trade policy. Similarly, a policy in Yugoslavia would not likely be successful if every country simply carried out its own foreign policy with little attention to the policies of the others. Pursuit of one's own goals would soon conflict with those of others and undermine the success of independent policymaking.

On the other hand, if states pool their resources and cooperate, they may enhance their impact at the cost of compromising their objectives. These seem to be the alternatives somewhat starkly presented: either dilute one's objectives by blending them into common positions or pursue goals independently but at the cost of a common voice and effectiveness. In a world where states are not heavily dependent on one another, unilateral foreign policy may be utilized. However, the greater the interdependence, the less the chance of successfully pursuing one's own goals in isolation from others, and the more states will rely on multilateral solutions.

Much of the discussion about CFSP in the EU centers on institutions. Where do institutions fit into this picture? If all members of the EU agreed on what to do, for example, in the Middle East, the Gulf War, and the Yugoslav crisis, few institutions for foreign policy coordination would be necessary. An automatic consensus ("harmony") would exist, based on the convergence of preferences among the member states. On the other hand, if everyone disagreed strongly, and it was not possible to negotiate a common position, institutions would be irrelevant, since institutions by themselves cannot make conflictual relations harmonious.

Institutions may make cooperation possible, by facilitating coordination, without succumbing to the fallacy of believing that for every problem there is an institutional solution. This is worth remembering because many students of the EU seem to think that the major problems of the CFSP can be solved by inventing a new procedure or rule. But if the United Kingdom, France, Italy, and Germany have widely different interests in Kosovo or Bosnia, then there is little that institutional engineering can do. To summarize, Europe is not ineffectual because it does not have a single phone number. Rather, it does not have a single phone number because of widely different goals and historical traditions of foreign policy-making. Since the foreign policy goals of the member states are critical to developing a CFSP, I start with a brief examination of the national interests (or goals) of some important member states.

National Interests of Member States

Three of the most important member states of the EU, Germany, France, and the United Kingdom, have interests that sometimes come together and sometimes diverge. Germany is the largest of the member states, with a population of over 80 million people and the largest economy in Europe. The successful operation of the German economy is important for the overall economic health of the EU. At the same time, Germany's role in the EU is restricted by its historical past and by fears that it will once again become too powerful.

Germany's geographical position is also the source of some disquiet. Germany has occupied a geopolitical position in the center of Europe, between East and West during the Cold War, and before that between France, Italy, the Netherlands, and Belgium in the West and Poland and Russia to the East. The *Mittellage*, or "middle condition," refers to this precarious geopolitical position. While this geographical position meant one thing under the balance of power system, its significance has changed in the contemporary world where Germany is thoroughly anchored within the institutions of the Atlantic Alliance and the EU. Nevertheless, Germany is a pivotal actor that has not pulled its full diplomatic weight in the past. Indeed, it has been difficult to even use the term national interest in Germany for fear of arousing anxiety among its neighbors.

Yet, Germany does have national interests even if it chooses to see its interests merging very closely with Europe as a whole. German citizens, firms, and state leaders have been anxious to present themselves as good Europeans committed to the integration project (Katzenstein 1997, 13–19). The Deutschmark, Germany's currency, is a source of national pride. Thus, in the negotiations leading up to Economic and Monetary Union, Germany was firm in preserving key elements of the national banking and financial system, most notably the independent central bank. Two principal European goals of Germany are assuring price stability at the regional level and increasing the ties between Germany and countries in Central and Eastern Europe.

Arguably, France has been the most important actor in the EU. The Benelux countries are too small and do not really form a bloc; Italy has been racked by internal divisions and unstable governments; and Germany, the great "civilian power," cannot, for a variety of historical reasons, play a bigger role than it has. This leaves France, a middle power with a history of great power status, skilled in the ways of international diplomacy, and desirous of playing a large role in world politics. French support, even leadership, has been crucial for almost all initiatives within the EU (agriculture, European Political Cooperation, monetary policy), and France has been an important, if difficult, partner within the NATO. If a counterweight to the role of the United States in world politics is to come about, it will almost certainly have to be based on a strong French role.

Although France was defeated and occupied by Germany during World War II, it came out as a victorious power. France occupied a seat as a permanent member of the Security Council of the United Nations (one of five Great Powers) and exerted surprisingly strong leverage within the NATO after it was formed in 1949 (Vernet 1992, 31). Because of dissatisfaction with American hegemony within the integrated military command structures of the NATO, France withdrew from these structures and pursued its own *force de frappe* (independent nuclear strike force). More than any other country within the NATO, France sought independence from the United States. It was willing to pay the price of incurring the displeasure of not only the United States but also other European countries.

The bipolar structure of the international system, with the United States and the Soviet Union as superpowers, each with its well-marked sphere of influence in Europe, suited France's ambitions (Vernet 1992, 31). For one thing, this structure clearly identified friend and foe, and made it all but impossible for the United States to defend Europe while at the same time putting France at the mercies of the Warsaw Pact. If the United States was to deter a nuclear attack against Western Europe, it could not let bombs drop on Paris while preventing their flight to Frankfurt, Rome, and London. In addition, the division of Germany between East and West made for a weaker Germany, and ensured French influence over a Federal Republic that was at the same time geographically truncated and under political wraps.

Many of the factors that made for French preeminence have changed. Germany is reunited, the Cold War is over, and the Warsaw Treaty Organization has been disbanded. In addition, the EU is now composed of fifteen members instead of the original six. With the expansion eastward and northward, Germany's influence is likely to expand. Austria, Finland, and Sweden joined in January of 1995 and Poland, Hungary, and the Czech Republic will likely be next. France no longer has a special hold on Germany, nor is it inconceivable that the EU could take some bold new initiative without France. Thus, France has to develop policies to pursue its interests in a very new Community setting. As the foreign minister of France, Alain Juppé, pointed out in 1993, "Germany, with its 80 million people and an economy that will have digested the problems of reunification within three or four years, will have a substantial sphere of influence in Central and Eastern Europe, stretching to the Ukraine and all the way to Russia, and it may be tempted to say that it needs European integration far less than it did 20 years ago. This temptation exists and we have to face it" (cited in Menon 1996).

What this dilemma regarding Germany implies for France is a sharper trade-off between a strong leadership role in the EU and the pursuit of national autonomy. The French have been quite adept at preserving the national veto in important decisions while at the same time building coalitions to move the process of integration ahead (Menon 1996, 248–249). However, the choices for France are becoming more constrained. It is likely that in the years ahead France will have to make a choice to accept German style institutional commitments (more reliance on majority voting, greater movement toward a true CFSP) or else lose control over the direction and pace of the integration process.

The United Kingdom joined the EU late (in 1973). It chose not to join the original EEC, opting to stay out and attempting instead to organize its relations within the European Free Trade Association (EFTA), a much looser economic organization with no supranational ambitions. Later, in 1963, the British application for membership was vetoed by President de Gaulle who had a variety of reasons for keeping the British out. Whatever de Gaulle's motives, it cannot be denied that the UK immediately stands out as very different from the other members of the EU. Geographically, the UK is separated from the Continent by twenty miles of English Channel. This geographic isolation contributes to a feeling of isolation from the Continent, illustrated by the fictional British newspaper headline which reads: "Fog Over Channel: Continent Isolated." With today's technology, twenty miles means little in terms of transportation and communication, but there is a lot of history (of conflict, wars, separation) that is represented by this short stretch of water.

The United Kingdom's position has meant that it has operated internationally within a different set of networks, comprised of the Commonwealth and the Atlantic area. Until perhaps the late sixties, the Commonwealth and the Atlantic were more important. Although the UK's ties to Western Europe have strengthened, and ties to the EFTA countries, the Commonwealth, and the United States have weakened relatively, it still is subject to a different set of forces than France, Italy, and Germany, the bulk of whose economic activities are centered in Europe.

The UK's behavior within the EU has been predictable. The British have been an awkward partner (George 1997), far from the most enthusiastic of members. They have dragged their feet on social policy, refusing to sign the social chapter of the Treaty on European Union, and they have refused to join EMU, though Prime Minister Tony Blair is keeping his options open for the future. In addition, the UK has been a vigorous critic of the common agricultural policy (CAP), especially its pricing policies, and has consistently opposed the transfer of power to institutions in Brussels.

However, the UK was in favor of the Single European Act (SEA) which instituted the single market by 1993. The SEA outlined a deregulatory project for expanding and perfecting the internal market that was very much in line with the UK's domestic agenda. This demonstrates, once again, that cooperation will occur within the EU when member states agree on the basic objectives that are being pursued. A pro-European solution is not expected to occur just to please other members, while stifling the goals and interests of cooperating countries. Governments are elected to represent certain interests and constituencies, not to pursue some abstract notion of cooperation. I make this point simply to emphasize that institutions, however effective, must start with the interests of states as raw material, and must try to devise solutions that take divergent interests into account.

In sum, the UK has defined its interests in terms of retaining full powers and sovereignty for the member states. This has meant insisting on the use of the veto. The UK also would like to build a market at the European level that is not heavily regulated and that does not bring along with it extensive social obligations, such as social security requirements, unemployment insurance, maternity leave allowances and so forth. Margaret Thatcher's infamous speech in Bruges in 1988 emphasized the opportunities afforded by extending free market principles to the regional level at the same time that it warned of the dangers of transferring sovereignty to Brussels. Thus, Thatcher pursued a transnational market but a national political system and national culture. While the Labour government under Tony Blair has changed the emphasis somewhat, the UK still strongly values national sovereignty and the market.

In sum, the interests of the member states can be quite different. The role of institutions in forging common policies based on different interests is taken up in the next section.

Institutional Development of the CFSP

The Rome Treaty, which established the EEC, had few provisions for the coordination of foreign policies. Presumably, foreign policies were to be made by the individual nation-states, according to their own procedures. If particular countries wanted to coordinate their policies bilaterally or even multilaterally, they were of course free to do so, but there was to be no burden or presumption that states would do so. This omission was not an accident. Functionalists, employing the "Community method" (integrationist, supranationalist) wanted to avoid areas of "high politics" which included foreign policy and especially defense and security policy. And representatives of national governments, whom we can call intergovernmentalists, wanted to preserve autonomy for the nation-states in the making of foreign policy.

Charles de Gaulle led France at the time the EEC came into existence. A staunch advocate of preserving powers of the nation-states, de Gaulle saw the need for political cooperation, but he insisted that this cooperation take place within a framework that respected the authority and independence of the states. To his mind, the nation-states were the only real source of authority in the world. Only their representatives were duly elected and charged with carrying out a mandate. The institutions of the EEC were creatures of states. They could be convenient vehicles for carrying out aspects of state policy, but they could never be independent. Only the nation-states could be the ultimate guardians of national projects and only they could set domestic agendas and make policy.

As a result of his worldview, de Gaulle set up the Fouchet Committee in 1960. He intended it to be a mechanism for foreign policy coordination, a sort of political directorate that allowed the member states of the EEC to discuss their foreign policies and to formulate common positions. It was a loose, very decentralized approach to foreign policy coordination that required almost no sacrifice to the autonomy of the member states. This Committee ceased to exist after 1962 (Piening 1997, 332).

During the sixties, there was little effort to move the integration process along in the security area. The EEC was still in its infancy and was preoccupied with establishing a free trade area, customs union, and a common agricultural policy. The Gaullist agenda dominated until 1969 when de Gaulle, weakened by earlier events of May 1968 (riots, student unrest), resigned the French presidency. His resignation allowed the reappearance of certain things on the political agenda, including the expansion of the EC and a reexamination of the role of the Community in the world. The Hague Summit of 1969, and the Luxembourg Report of the following year, called for close scrutiny of these related issues. Further, the Luxembourg Report set out a scheme for meetings and cooperation at several levels, including periodic European summits, foreign ministers meetings within the EPC, and meetings of working groups among mid-level and junior officials (Dinan 1994, 468).

The Hague Summit and Luxembourg Report established the system of European Political Cooperation (EPC), an informal procedure for cooperating in the area of foreign policy. In some ways, the EPC was not so different from the Fouchet Committee, though the EPC was not the product of any one country's vision. Nevertheless, it was a very decentralized set of procedures. As Michael Smith points out, "In terms of formal rules, EPC was not linked to the EC, not supported by a permanent organization or bureaucracy, and not even negotiated as a treaty. It had no permanent budget or staff for many years, no resources of its own, no meeting place, no secretariat-general or chief official, and no specific areas of competence" (Smith 1998, 307). But like the Conference on Security and Cooperation in Europe (CSCE, which became the OSCE in the mid-1990s), which for many years did not even have a postal address, it succeeded in paving the way to further integration and cooperation in the area of foreign policy.

The next big change in the institutionalization of procedures came with the passage of the SEA in 1986 and its coming into force in 1987. The SEA is best known for the creation of the single market. However, as Chris Piening points out (1997, 36), the "single" in the Single European Act refers to the fact that there is one treaty that integrates the changes needed to create the single market and the intergovernmental agreement on EPC. Title III of the SEA has to do with provisions for the coordination of foreign policies. Thus, for the first time, there is a legal instrument in the EU that establishes a basis for foreign policy cooperation. However, it is important to recognize that the actual basis of foreign policy cooperation was still very much decentralized and very much in the mold of EPC.

As Michael Smith points out, the SEA codified current practices and put them on a legal basis, essentially taking what was "soft law" (based on custom and accepted procedures) and putting them on a "hard law" (treaty-based) foundation (Smith 1998, 324). This gave a bit more precision and certainty to cooperation in the security area and nationalized some procedures, for example, the practice of treating the foreign ministers meeting in EPC as different from the foreign ministers meeting as the Council of Ministers.

Although the SEA moved things forward at a strictly legal level, it did not alter much the level of coordination among the key actors in making foreign policy. The system established by SEA was still very decentralized, lowest-common-denominator decisionmaking. The new legal basis did little to change the ineffectual responses of the EC to challenges posed by the Soviet invasion of Afghanistan in 1979, the ongoing conflict in the Middle East, or the United States invasion of Grenada in 1983. Nor did any coherent conception of foreign policy guide the European member states in preparing for the reunification of Germany and the collapse of the Soviet Union. However, with the end of the Cold War and the anticipated changes in Eastern Europe, France became convinced that stronger foreign policy coordination would be needed (Gordon 1997/1998, 85), not only to respond to Eastern Europe and a dissolving Soviet Union, but also to bind Germany more closely to European institutions.

Whereas the pressures for greater institutional integration came partly from political events in the external world, there was also pressure from the EC itself, that is, pressure to develop cooperation in foreign policy as a way of keeping up with even more rapid integration advances in monetary policy. In 1989 the European Council decided to launch another Intergovernmental Conference (IGC) on Economic and Monetary Union (EMU). Many officials in the EC expressed the belief that substantial advances in EMU, without companion changes in other areas (citizenship rights, environment, foreign policy), would create too great an imbalance between the economic and foreign policy capacities of the EU. Thus, and in light of the prospect of German reunification as discussed above, the IGC on monetary union was expanded to include a second IGC on political union.

The result of these two IGCs was the Treaty on European Union (TEU), which was signed at Maastricht, the Netherlands, in 1991 and which entered into force in 1993. The TEU creates a three-pillar structure (see Chapter 3, Figure 3.4). The first pillar incorporates the older EC treaties, now amended to include EMU. Business conducted under this pillar takes place according to the rules of EC institutions; that is, the Commission, the Council of Ministers, the European Parliament and the ECJ all continue to play their traditional roles. The second pillar is Common Foreign and Security Policy (CFSP), and the third pillar is Justice and Home Affairs (JHA). The second and third pillars are outside the EC but are part of the European Union. The distinction is important because decision-making in the area of foreign and security policy does not take place according to the same rules (for example, voting rules) that apply in other issue areas. Consensus among governments is still required.

However, the CFSP is not simply a more treaty-based version of EPC. As Piening puts it, "The CFSP places the Council at the heart of the process. The Union is represented in foreign affairs by the presidency (Article J.5), the same presidency that deals with all other Community business.[2] The Commission is 'fully associated with the work carried out in the common foreign and security policy field' (Article J.9). The European Parliament is consulted on 'the main aspects and the basic choices' of the CFSP, and the presidency is to take its views into consideration" (Piening 1997, 39).

These institutional changes by themselves do not create foreign policy cooperation. In the end, they are changes in the legal and regulatory environment within which states conduct foreign policymaking. The changes are intended to rationalize decisionmaking, to enhance the exchange of views, to facilitate common analyses, and to provide the means to cooperate if common interests exist or can be forged. Two things are striking from the above description of institutionalization of procedures in CFSP. The first is that it proved difficult and in the end impossible to separate "high politics" (defense, security) from "low politics" (economics, functional cooperation). It is difficult to imagine that the advances in CFSP would have occurred if the single market had not been completed and monetary union successfully launched. The second remarkable thing is that, with hindsight, there seems to have occurred an inevitable tendency for the procedures of EPC to become entwined with EC procedures. Despite all attempts to completely insulate these two institutional domains, there was "institutional creep" between the Council of Ministers, the Commission, and the foreign ministers meeting in EPC.

Development of the Substance of a CFSP

The successful development of a common foreign policy, including security policy, cannot be judged solely by the procedures and institutions created to facilitate cooperation. One can easily imagine an intricate framework of rules and institutions that have little effect on the actual level of cooperation. Indeed, some critics have taken the United States and the EU to task for focusing too much on the procedural side and too little on the substantive side (Zelikow 1996). For example, Zelikow criticized the former U.S. Assistant Secretary of State for European Affairs, Richard Holbrooke, for emphasizing the "new security architecture" of Europe while the EU failed to come up with a policy to deal with the deadly crisis in Yugoslavia. Indeed, Holbrooke himself considered the war in Bosnia to be a great failure of collective security, perhaps the biggest failure since the 1930s when Italy defied the League of Nations and invaded Ethiopia. Yet, at the same time, Holbrooke focused his energies on building the institutions for making foreign policy rather than the foreign policy itself (Zelikow 1996, 7).

At best, institutions can facilitate the making of cooperative foreign policy. If the national interests of states are taken as given, the existence of institutions may make it easier to cooperate by making information available, by making interactions more transparent, by monitoring behavior to assure that the members comply, and by helping to overcome collective action problems. If states fundamentally disagree on what their interests are, or even on what strategy to follow, there is little that common institutions can do to solve the problem. Institutions can even worsen the problem, and make cooperation more difficult, by putting rules in place that make it harder to achieve a common policy. Within the EU, the requirement that all the states—not just the major states, or a crucial sub-set of states—agree on matters of security cooperation before common action can be undertaken, hinders the capacity of less than universal coalitions to take action. If during the Gulf War, the demanding procedures of

Maastricht had been in place, France and the United Kingdom might have had a more difficult time forming a coalition with the United States, since they would have been required to search for a consensus among themselves (Zelikow 1996, 9–10).

FOREIGN POLICY CHALLENGES

To understand the substance of Europe's foreign policy, I will examine three important episodes in which there was a foreign policy challenge, that is, some international pressure that called for a collective response: the price increases of oil by the Organization of Petroleum Exporting Countries (OPEC) in 1973; the Gulf War of 1990–1991; and the wars in Yugoslavia from 1991 to 1999.

OPEC Oil Price Increases

When the OPEC countries announced their quadrupling of the price of oil in October of 1973, the initial response of the EC countries was simply confusion and disarray. While the action took place against the background of war in the Middle East, and reflected Arab desire to retaliate against European supporters of Israel, EC members were taken by surprise. The second stage was not cooperative problem solving but rather the search for bilateral deals. To some extent, the Europeans allowed themselves to be divided by OPEC's designation of certain countries as "friendly" and others as "unfriendly." France was designated as "friendly" and Germany and the Netherlands (the most pro-Israeli country) were termed "unfriendly." This policy reinforced existing cleavages in the EC and did not help in finding areas of agreement. So the French signed long-term contracts with Saudi Arabia in exchange for arms and industrial know-how, Italy cooperated with Libya for special privileges, and West Germany tried a number of options, including greater cooperation with its European partners and with the United States (Kohl 1976, 92).

Europeans could be forgiven for not immediately reacting with a common policy in response to the embargo and price increases. After all, by 1973 the EC had only been in existence for fifteen years and had focused almost all of its attention during the first decade and a half on completing the customs union and common agricultural policy. The informal process of European Political Cooperation (EPC) had barely begun (1970), and there was little by way of expectations, rules, and common institutions to facilitate a joint response. After the initial disarray, there was an attempt at a coherent common response. However, this response was weakened from the very beginning by pressures from below (the member states) and outside (the United States). On November 6, 1973, the EC passed a resolution calling for Israeli withdrawal from the territories occupied by them. This collective response provoked a negative reaction from the United States, who strongly supported Israel. In December, Henry Kissinger, secretary of state at the time, delivered his famous speech in London, taking Europeans to task for attempting "to elevate refusal to consult into a principle defining European identity" (Kissinger 1973, 575; reprinted in Kissinger, *American Foreign Policy*). After the Kissinger speech, the EC members met in Copenhagen to try to hammer out the broad framework for cooperation regarding energy policy, but this effort was largely a failure (Prodi and Clô 1975, 106).

The final stage of the European response to the oil crisis involved the internationalization of the European effort, or the merging of the European response with that of the United States. The Washington Energy Conference in 1974 began the process of incorporating the EC effort into a wider international response, though one controlled by the United States. This Conference led to the establishment of the Energy Coordinating Group, which included eight of nine members of the EC (France did not join officially, but the United Kingdom, Ireland, and Denmark were EC members by this time) plus the United States, Canada, Japan, and Norway.

The EC countries were divided in terms of resource potential (the Netherlands had large gas deposits, the United Kingdom had North Sea oil), outside ties (the French had good ties with several Middle East countries, Italy with Libya), and historical legacies (the Germans took a strong anti-inflationary stance, the French emphasized full employment). These cleavages worked against a strong collective response. National sovereignty and national interests were paramount. Countries explored the possibilities of common policies but were not ready to sacrifice their own interests for the sake of a common position.

The Gulf War

When Saddam Hussein of Iraq invaded Kuwait on August 2, 1990, the response of the United States was swift. President Bush ordered the Iraqi troops out and set a deadline for their withdrawal. For the EC countries, the invasion coincided with many other important things on the agenda, including the end of the Cold War, the impending reunification of Germany, and negotiations about monetary and political union, the subjects of two Intergovernmental Conferences (IGCs). Since the Maastricht Treaty was not yet in existence, the foreign ministers of the EC met in EPC and immediately condemned the invasion and imposed economic sanctions. However, the member states were completely unable to come up with a coherent response about how to deal with the crisis militarily. A group of members of the European Parliament was dispatched to the region, and they met with various heads of state, but not with much effect. For his part, Saddam Hussein refused even to meet with an EC delegation, considering it powerless to act under these circumstances. Once again, the response to this problem in the Middle East took shape along global lines, with the United States leading the way, and with various European countries deciding for themselves how they ought to respond (Piening 1997, 76).

Two IGCs were taking place while the Gulf War was ongoing. The first had to do with monetary unification. This IGC led to the provisions of the Maastricht Treaty for monetary unification and provided the foundation for the movement to the Euro (the European single currency) in 1999. The other conference, more controversial, had to do with political union, including greater unification of foreign and security policy. This IGC had the difficult task of making the transition from EPC to CFSP. Although some members of the Commission were optimistic about making this transition, it proved premature. Indeed, as French Foreign Minister Roland Dumas remarked in January 1991, the Gulf War had demonstrated "that Europe does not have a common foreign policy" (quoted in Dinan 1994, 470).

Why did the EC fail to respond with a coherent foreign policy in the Gulf War? One could criticize the lack of cooperation, or blame a "failure of will," or attribute the problem to the imperfect EC foreign policy making machinery. But in the end, the member countries did not act together (that is, did not cooperate) because they did not have the same interests, nor interests that could be shaped and compromised so as to become an acceptable package to all. Different national interests, different domestic priorities, and sovereign decisionmaking rules produced different responses. The United Kingdom, represented by Thatcher, who happened to be in the United States at the time, immediately sided with the United States and promised to follow through with military help. The Germans, deeply preoccupied with reunification, and historically discouraged from carrying out military activities in any case, supported the anti-Hussein cause with financial aid, but did not send troops. If Germany had done so, around the time reunification was taking place, it would certainly have raised the anxiety levels of many other European countries. Germany had to lie low and remain inconspicuous, and yet it was expected to help in some way. The French did contribute to the U.S. led coalition, but only after an initial period when France displayed considerably greater pro-diplomacy sympathies (Dinan 1994, 470–471).

The Conflict in Yugoslavia

To many observers, Yugoslavia has always been a simmering cauldron of ethnic and religious rivalries. Yugoslavia was formed out of the collapse of the Ottoman and Austro-Hungarian Empires after World War I. Its republics—Croatia, Macedonia, Montenegro, Serbia, Slovenia, and Bosnia-Herzogovina—were based on religious and ethnic lines, though many republics had significant minorities within them. Yugoslavia represented a compromise between two opposing forces, not easy to reconcile, of national self-determination and power politics. The former provided a principle for nations to organize themselves into separate states; the latter cautioned that states had to be large and powerful enough to be viable players in the game of international politics.

After World War II, two factors conspired to support Yugoslavia's role in the international system. The first factor was the person of Marshall Tito. Tito was a remarkable leader who carefully balanced the separatist forces in Yugoslavia. Tito was a Communist, so when he came to power in 1945, it was natural for him to shift the focus to class conflict. One of the core beliefs of communism, that class conflict was central, happened to coincide with Tito's desire to discourage nationalism among the separate groups. Thus, he never sought to fan the fires of national feelings or to play to the potentially explosive histories of the different peoples in this part of the world. The second factor was the bipolar power structure in Europe after 1945. As soon as the war ended, the United States and the Soviet Union organized into two hostile camps, and each side subsequently formed its own military and economic organizations. This tight bipolarity provided an overall power structure that discouraged the expression of conflict and of separatism. The Soviet Union would not permit the secession of Slovenia and Croatia and their association with the EEC, or even allow them to play a neutral role in the manner of Austria or Sweden.

Marshall Tito died in May of 1980, but Yugoslavia did not fall apart until a decade later, and then only when the collapse of the Soviet Union and the end of the Cold War were imminent. Although the collapse of the Soviet Union was a necessary condition for secession, pressures within Yugoslavia among the Republics go back to the sixties and seventies (Gagnon 1994/1995, 142).

If the end of the Cold War was a necessary condition for outbreak of war, it was not sufficient. The trigger mechanism was provided by the secession of Croatia and Slovenia in June of 1991. Germany was quick to recognize these Republics as states whereas several other EC states, as well as the United States, were reluctant to do so. Indeed, the United States was quite firm in its desire to see Yugoslavia stay together as one country. When Slovenia seceded, Serbia (the dominant Republic in Yugoslavia) immediately went to war, but suffered a quick defeat. The war spread first to Croatia, later to Bosnia-Herzegovina, and most recently to Kosovo. During the last stage of this violent conflict, in Kosovo, the

NATO got heavily involved and carried out a seventy-eight day bombing campaign before Serbian troops withdrew from Kosovo.

What was the EC response in Yugoslavia? Its first response, before the fighting actually broke out, was to support the territorial integrity of the country. This should not be surprising. The institution of sovereignty is built upon the idea of mutual recognition among member states and support of existing borders. The international system could hardly function fluidly if states constantly tried to undermine the borders of other states. Thus, at their summit in Rome in 1990, the heads of government resolutely called for the maintenance of the territorial integrity of Yugoslavia (Dinan 1994, 484). However, this proved to be a difficult position to maintain in the face of challenges among several Republics to form their own state. Demands for independence increased, and these demands were reinforced by rumors of hostilities as well as by popular referenda that gave testimony to the broad support the cause of independence enjoyed (Dinan 1994, 484). It was difficult for the EC to portray itself as the champion of democracy in the new Europe at the same time that it backed antidemocratic forces in Yugoslavia.

Less than a year later, the EC found itself much more sympathetic to the Slovenian and Croatian causes. In June of 1991, shortly after fighting broke out in Yugoslavia, the Community sent a troika of foreign ministers on a mission to Belgrade to attempt to defuse the fighting. This was a highly ambitious international diplomatic *démarche*, and it provided some visibility to the EC's foreign policy dimension. By acting together, the EC gave reason for others to take it more seriously.

However, cleavages soon surfaced. As mentioned, Germany pushed hard for recognition of Croatia and Slovenia, and other member states felt unduly pressured. Quite apart from the merits of eventual independence, France felt that the timing was unwise, in that minorities within Croatia and Slovenia, and the other Republics, were unprotected. It would be far better to work out a comprehensive arrangement to assure the rights of minorities everywhere in Yugoslavia, within an overall settlement that involved international peacekeepers from the start, before the fighting broke out. However, the EC as a whole recognized Croatia in January 1992, and subsequently recognized Slovenia and Bosnia also. But this joint recognition could not hide the fact that the member states had different positions. Mitterrand, the president of France, left an EC summit in June of 1992 to secretly visit Sarajevo in an effort to find a solution to the fighting there (Dinan 1994, 487). The timing could hardly have been worse. Mitterrand had just taken part in high-level meetings in the EC where the need to coordinate and communicate in the foreign policy area was discussed extensively, but then he proceeded to engage in unilateral diplomacy.

While EU countries eventually contributed money and military personnel to Yugoslavia, they did so most effectively within the context of the leadership and support of NATO. Considered as a foreign policy unit itself, the EU was ineffective. The Germans, who played an initial role in recognition of breakaway Republics, did not want to contribute militarily, even within NATO, since Yugoslavia represented an "out-of-area" operation. The French had strong historical ties to Serbia and were not as reflexively opposed to them as the British or the Americans. Italy, a close neighbor, did not want to stir up trouble and was fearful of refugees as well as damage to its tourism industry. While the United Kingdom was strongly supportive of NATO-backed action that included the United States, it still opted for the most decentralized form of foreign policymaking within the EU.

SUMMARY

Overall, the EU has not fared well in the construction of a Common Foreign and Security Policy in Yugoslavia. One of its members (Germany) helped to trigger the crisis by premature recognition of Slovenia and Croatia, and the EC did little to stop the cascade of insecurities that followed this recognition. Its efforts to mediate, sometimes unilateral and sometimes multilateral, ended mostly in failure. The EU's weak showing in Yugoslavia is mirrored in its failure to forge a successful collective response in other areas, from the OPEC oil embargo of the 1970s to the most recent events of the nineties. French unilateralism persists in the intervention in Rwanda in 1994 as well as in subsequent nuclear tests carried out by the French in 1995, tests that were vigorously opposed by eleven of the fifteen member states of the EU (Gordon 1997/1998, 88). The British, much more willing to cooperate with global (U.S.-led) efforts in the Gulf and in Yugoslavia, have been among the most reluctant to create stronger institutions for a shared foreign policy. At another level, Greece still obstructs Turkey's application for EU membership as well as Macedonian recognition. France and Germany together have shown their unwillingness to back an EU resolution critical of China's human rights record for fear that it might endanger economic dealings with Beijing (Gordon 1997/1998, 88).

The EU's incoherence in foreign policy is reflected in its limited capacity for joint military action on a broad scale. To be sure, this may already be due to the absence of collective will in the first place. Europe certainly has the resources—the people, the control over raw materials, the industrial capacity—to create serious military strength if it so desires. One could argue that military incapacity stems from the absence of a serious will to project forces and respond to external challenges in a unified way, rather than the other way around. Still, it is interesting to consider whether a small part of Europe's problem is supply-side, dependent on resources and capability. Europe is still highly dependent militarily on NATO: for equipment, intelligence, long-distance cargo capacity, and sophisticated aerial surveillance. As Gordon points out, intelligence (data gathering and analysis) remains a national prerogative (Gordon 1997/1998, 88) and most of the forces within the individual NATO countries (well over two million just within the Western European Union) are trained, supported, and organized around defense of the respective homelands. Outside of France and the United Kingdom, there is very little capacity to lift personnel and materiel, to carry them long distances, and to project forces far outside the borders of the country. There is little sign that this is changing. EU countries spend little on defense (slightly above 2 percent of GDP) and are already counting on the "peace dividend" to reduce spending further (Gordon 1997/1998, 93). With sluggish economic growth, pressures to divert resources from defense to investment will increase. Thus, the prospects for a more adequate military capacity are not likely to improve.

The problem of constructing a shared foreign policy is at bottom a problem of building first a foundation of common interests. Shared interests in the security field are not likely to emerge spontaneously as a result of rubbing elbows in common institutions. The stakes are too great, the histories and domestic agendas of the members too divergent, and the outside ties, especially to the United States, impinge differently on the key EU actors. When interests are different and the actors are sovereign, states will be reluctant to give up their independence to further an abstract cause of European unity. Why should foreign policy reflect common positions when common positions do not exist on the ground? The question inevitably has to be raised: whose common position?

A price has to be paid for non-cooperation, and that price is paid in the currency of influence. To the extent that EU members do not forge a cooperative stance, they retain their individual autonomy but give up impact and influence. This is the fundamental trade-off, or dilemma, and it is usually decided in favor of autonomy. If every country in the EU could have the impact it desires, of course, a common policy would be unproblematic. But this is just the difficulty. If all cooperate, the EU has a greater impact and can influence events, but the direction of this influence is not what some of the members want. Thus, they go it alone.

To alter the present stalemate in CFSP, countries would have to agree to cede some sovereignty in the way decisions are made, making it possible to decide without the agreement of all. But the structure of decision-making is not likely to change in the direction of greater supranationality. What this would mean in practice is greater reliance on qualified majority voting (QMV) in the Council of Ministers on crucial foreign policy questions. This is where the foreign ministers of the member states meet. It would also have to mean that less of the business of foreign policy gets conducted in the European Council, where heads of state meet.

France strictly adheres to the use of the Council of Ministers and to the use of unanimity in important areas. France is willing to discuss extending QMV to areas that are either not too important or subject to French control. Thus, the French combine discussions of extending QMV with a re-weighting of the votes in the Council in order to give France greater veto power if it wants to prevent action (Menon 1996, 244–245). The British continue to support intergovernmental arrangements. Indeed, it was the British and the French who insisted that CFSP be located under Pillar 2 of the Maastricht Treaty, so as to keep it separate from the Community institutions (the Commission, the Parliament, and the ECJ). Neither did the reunification of Germany propel the United Kingdom and France along a common trajectory. One interpretation of the reunification of Germany is that it encouraged greater integration, particularly on the part of France, which saw closer ties to Germany as the only option after the five Eastern *Länder* joined with the Federal Republic. France thus moved from a position of balancing Germany (keeping Germany weaker) to cementing Germany more firmly into Europe (Moravcsik 1998, 418). Whatever the merits of this argument, German reunification did not move Germany, France, and the United Kingdom closer together. Only in Germany had basic national identity changed enough to commit itself to deeper integration in the area of foreign policy (Katzenstein 1997, 33).

The Amsterdam Treaty, signed in 1997 with the shortcomings of the second pillar in mind but without any pressing conflicts generating pressure for change, did little to change CFSP. The European Commission won the right to submit proposals to the member states, but states are under no obligation to consider, less still to accept, those proposals. Decisionmaking procedures remain driven by unanimity, although "constructive abstention" is allowed. Article 23 (ex-Article J.13), nominally allows for qualified majority voting in adopting narrow implementing decisions or joint actions, but the conditions for calling a vote are farcical. Article 23(2)(2) establishes that "If a member of the Council declares that, for important and stated reasons of national policy, it intends to oppose the adoption of a decision to be taken by qualified majority, a vote shall not be taken. The Council may, acting by a qualified majority, request that the matter be referred to the European Council for decision by unanimity." The net effect of this provision is that "voting" will only take place where unanimity exists! These and other provisions confirm Duff's assessment that provisions in CFSP in the Amsterdam Treaty represent a "crafty illusion" (Duff 1997, 124).

Member states of the EU vary in their commitment to the European cause but all—Germany the least perhaps, the United Kingdom the most—greatly value their sovereignty and autonomy. Margaret Thatcher was the most vocal in defending the value of sovereignty, but she no doubt spoke for some of the others when she gave her famous Bruges speech in 1988, where she argued that certain essential functions lie at the heart of the sovereign nation-state, among them monetary, fiscal, and foreign policy. Her speech made clear that British sovereignty was the important issue and that "we (the British) have surrendered enough" (cited in Moravcsik 1998, 419). Sovereignty, the ultimate right to decide one's fate, is still very much alive in Europe today. As long as it endures, and as long as the member states represent different interests, Europe is not likely to have an effective Common Foreign and Security Policy.

CONCLUSION

In this chapter, I have explored three aspects of the external relations of the EU: its closed-open nature, the presumed trade-off between widening and deepening, and the tug and pulls of sovereign nation-states attempting to create a Common Foreign and Security Policy. Since all three aspects are presented as dilemmas, there is no expectation that they will be resolved in any final sense. Rather, they are enduring tensions we can only hope to better appreciate.

The relations between Europe and the rest of the world have often been thought of in narrow economic terms, as if it were all a question of how well the EU fits with the GATT or its successor the World Trade Organization. Economics is certainly important but so are politics and culture. Europe's emerging forms of democratic governance, its devices for assuring limitations on the exercise of power, the changing relationships among courts, parliaments, and executives, patterns of interest group influence, and conceptions of citizenship are also important. Indeed, applicant states from Central and Eastern Europe must not only adapt to the economic requirements of market capitalism; they must also demonstrate convergence with the political criteria set forth for accession. Culture, while rarely mentioned, is surely important. The Turkish application for membership—on the table since the mid-1960s!—has been treated differently from those of other states not just because of Turkey's human rights record, but also because it is an Islamic country. Whether the EU could tolerate an Islamic country among its members, as opposed to an Islamic state, only time will tell.

What about the relationship between regional unity in Europe and a more comprehensive world government? From the Hague Peace Conferences in 1899 and 1907, to the League of Nations after World War I, to the United Nations after World War II, world government has been a lively part of the public debate. In the late forties, the world government movement spawned over seventy organizations around the world, with hundreds of thousands of members (Wagar 1963, 221). Philosophers and publicists, including Bertrand Russell, Julian Huxley, Arnold Toynbee, Pitirim Sorokin, F.C.S. Northrop, and Norman Cousins, supported or outlined proposals for world government. The Atlantic Union movement, strongly advocated by Clarence Streit, took its original geographical focus as only the beginning of a much wider integration of the rest of the world. By contrast, the EU will at most extend eastward to Ukraine (but not Russia), south to Cyprus and Malta (but not to North Africa), and southeast no further than Turkey.

The EU is not closed economically, but it is also not likely to become a cell in a more comprehensive world government. Still, if the EU can expand to twenty-five to thirty countries, live together peacefully, and prosper economically, while reaching out to the world in productive ways, it arguably will have made a contribution. Its past experience—expansion of membership, openness in its economic relations, development efforts in the less developed world—show that the EU is not a modern version of List's "closed commercial state," nor Rousseau's "isolated Corsica." However, the poor showing of the EU in Yugoslavia, and with regard to common foreign policy positions in general, indicates that the EU has a long way to go before it acts as a single unit with the rest of the world.

NOTES

1. Moravcsik argues convincingly that geopolitical factors were not the only ones operating, indeed that they were probably not even decisive. He points out that there was substantial support for monetary integration among the business community within Germany, though it is not clear that this support would have been higher for EMU compared to EMS. He argues that "the sequence of events in fact helps us to *dismiss* (italics in original) the possibility that linkage to German unification was decisive" (Moravcsik 1998, 397). However, it is easier to admit that many things may have been operating than to agree that geopolitical factors were not decisive. Since we are dealing with one set of events here, in which several factors are confounded, we cannot attribute variation in outcomes to distinctive causal factors, much as we would like to do so.

2. The presidency refers to the Council presidency, which rotates among member states every six months, is responsible for setting Council priorities, and also provides a "point country" for dealing with the EU in various external forums.

REFERENCES

Bhagwati, Jagdish. 1997. "From Fast to Nowhere." *Economist* 24 (October): 21–23.
Cameron, David R. 1992. "The 1992 Initiative: Causes and Consequences." In *Euro-Politics: Institutions and Policymaking in the "New" European Community*, edited by Alberta M. Sbragia. Washington, D.C.: The Brookings Institution.

Cheysson, Claude. 1997. "Defining Europe's Place in the World." In *What Global Role for the EU?* Brussels, Belgium: Philip Morris Institute for Public Policy Research.

Dahrendorf, Ralf. 1971. "Possibilities and Limits of a European Communities Foreign Policy." *The World Today* 26, no. 4 (April):141–150.

Dimitrova, Antoaneta. 1998. "The Role of the EU in the Process of Democratic Transition and Consolidation in Central and Eastern Europe." In *The European Union in a Changing World*, a selection of conference papers, September 19–20, 1996, Brussels. Luxembourg: Office of Official Publications of the European Communities.

Dinan, Desmond. 1994. *An Ever Closer Union?* Boulder, Colo.: Lynne Rienner Publishers.

_____. 1998. "Reflections on the IGCs." In *The State of the European Union: Deepening and Widening*, edited by Pierre-Henri Laurent and Marc Maresceau. Boulder, Colo.: Lynne Rienner Publishers.

_____. 1999. *An Ever Closer Union?* 2d ed. Boulder, Colo.: Lynne Rienner Publishers.

Duff, Andrew, ed. 1997. *The Treaty of Amsterdam: Text and Commentary*. London: Sweet & Maxwell for the Federal Trust.

Eurostat: Facts and Figures. 1997. Luxembourg: Official Publications of the European Communities.

Gagnon, V.P. 1994/1995. "Ethnic Nationalism and International Conflict: The Case of Serbia." *International Security* 19, no. 3:130–166.

George, Stephen. 1997. *An Awkward Partner: Britain in the European Community*. 2d ed. Oxford: Clarendon Press.

Gordon, Philip H. (1997/1998). "Europe's Uncommon Foreign Policy." *International Security* 22, no. 3 (Winter):74–100.

Grieco, Joseph M. 1994. "Variations in Regional Economic Institutions in Western Europe, East Asia, and the Americas: Magnitude and Sources." Durham, N.C.: Department of Political Science, Duke University.

Hogan, Michael J. 1984. "European Integration and the Marshall Plan." In *The Marshall Plan: A Retrospective*, edited by Stanley Hoffmann and Charles Maier. Boulder, Colo.: Westview Press.

Hosli, Madeleine O. 1993. "Admission of European Free Trade Association states to the European Community: effects on voting power in the European Community Council of Ministers." *International Organization* 47, no. 4 (Autumn): 629–643.

Huntington, Samuel P. 1993. "The Clash of Civilizations?" *Foreign Affairs* 72, no. 3 (Summer):22–49.

Kahler, Miles. 1995. *Regional Futures and Transatlantic Economic Relations*. New York: Council on Foreign Relations Press.

Katzenstein, Peter J. 1997. "United Germany in an Integrating Europe." In *Tamed Power: Germany in Europe*, edited by Peter J. Katzenstein. Ithaca, N.Y.: Cornell University Press.

Kerremans, Bart. 1998. "The Political and Institutional Consequences of Widening: Capacity and Control in an Enlarged Council." In *The State of the European*

Union: Deepening and Widening, edited by Pierre-Henri Laurent and Marc Maresceau. Boulder, Colo.: Lynne Rienner Publishers.

Kirchner, Emil, and Karen Williams. 1983. "The Legal, Political, and Institutional Implications of the Isoglucose Judgments 1980." *Journal of Common Market Studies* 22, no. 2 (December):173–191.

Kissinger, Henry A. 1973. "European Unity and Atlantic Community." Address to the Pilgrims of Great Britain, London, December 12, 1973.

Kohl, Wilfred L. 1976. "The United States, Western Europe, and the Energy Problem." *Journal of International Affairs* 30, no. 1 (Spring/Summer):81–96.

Krause, Lawrence B. 1968. *European Economic Integration and the United States.* Washington, D.C.: The Brookings Institution.

Kreinin, M.E. 1960. "The Outer Seven and European Integration." *The American Economic Review* 50, no. 3:371–376.

Leibfried, Stephan, and Paul Pierson, eds. 1995. *European Social Policy: Between Fragmentation and Integration.* Washington, D.C.: The Brookings Institution.

Mancini, F. Federico, and David T. Keeling. 1994. "Democracy and the European Court of Justice." *Modern Law Review* 57:175–190.

Marks, Gary (1992). "Structural Policy in the European Community," in Alberta M. Sbragia (ed.), *Europolitics: Institutions and Policymaking in the 'New' European Community.* Washington, D.C.: The Brookings Institution.

Marks, Gary, and Richard Haesly. 1996. "Thinking Through Territorial Identity in Europe with Reference to Some Evidence." Paper presented at the International Conference of Europeanists, Chicago, Ill.

Menon, Anand. 1996. "France and the IGC of 1996." *Journal of European Public Policy* 3, no. 2 (June):231–252.

Mitrany, David. 1930. "Pan-Europa—A Hope or a Danger?" *The Political Quarterly* 1, no. 4 (September-December):457–478.

_____. 1963. "Delusions of Regional Unity." In *Limits and Problems of European Integration,* edited by B. Landheer. The Hague: Martinus Nijhoff.

Moravcsik, Andrew. 1991. "Negotiating the Single European Act: national interests and conventional statecraft in the European Community." *International Organization* 45 (Winter):19–56.

_____. 1998. *The Choice for Europe: Social Purpose and State Power from Messina to Maastricht.* Ithaca, N.Y.: Cornell University Press.

Piening, Christopher. 1997. *Global Europe: The European Union in World Affairs.* Boulder, Colo.: Lynne Rienner Publishers.

Prodi, Romano, and Alberto Clô. 1975. "Europe." In "The Oil Crisis in Perspective." *Daedalus* 104, no. 4(Fall):91–112.

Rhodes, Carolyn, ed. 1998. *The European Union in the World Community.* Boulder, Colo.: Lynne Rienner Publishers.

Risse, Thomas. 1999. "A Europeanization of Nation-State Identities?" To appear in *Transforming Europe: Europeanization and Domestic Change,* edited by Maria Green Cowles, James Caporaso, and Thomas Risse. Ithaca, N.Y.: Cornell University Press.

Serfaty, Simon. 1999. *Memories of Europe's Future.* Washington, D.C.: Center for Strategic and International Studies.

Smith, Michael E. 1998. "Rules, Transgovernmentalism, and the Expansion of European Political Cooperation." In *European Integration and Supranational Governance*, edited by Wayne Sandholtz and Alec Stone Sweet. Oxford: Oxford University Press.

Stone Sweet, Alec, and James A. Caporaso. 1998. "From Free Trade to Supranational Polity: The European Court and Integration." In *European Integration and Supranational Governance*, edited by Wayne Sandholtz and Alec Stone Sweet. Oxford: Oxford University Press.

Tewes, Henning. 1998. "Between Deepening and Widening: Role Conflict in Germany's Enlargement Policy." *West European Politics* 21, no. 2 (April):117–133.

Thatcher, Margaret. 1995. *The Path to Power*. New York: HarperCollins.

Vernet, Daniel. 1992. "France in a New Europe." *The National Interest*, no. 29 (Fall):30–38.

Viner, Jacob. 1950. *The Customs Union Issue*. London: Carnegie Endowment for International Peace.

Wagar, W. Warren. 1963. *The City of Man*. Baltimore, Md.: Penguin Books.

Zelikow, Philip. 1996. "The Masque of Institutions." *Survival* 38, no. 1:6–18.

FIVE

□ □ □

Conclusion

Throughout this book, I have used dilemmas as a device for organizing the subject matter of European integration. Rarely do all good things go together. Yet sometimes they do, as the founding fathers of European integration fervently believed. Economic cooperation and prosperity were to lead to peace; economic integration was to lead to political integration (spillover); and economic and political integration in turn would lead to loyalty transfer from the nation-state to the emerging supranational federation. The functionalist spirit that permeated the European project posited a remarkable congruence between economics and politics as well as between the place where a function was performed and the object of one's loyalties. As more and more functions shifted from national capitols to Brussels, so would national loyalties shift.

However, it is also true that choices have to be made between different values, between different states of affairs that are all beneficial in some sense. We can think of democracy and efficiency, community and freedom, accountability and performance, and certain rights of individuals and the mobility of capital. The view of the world given to us by dilemmas forces us to think in terms of choices and trade-offs. Cost and choice are intimately related in the sense that choosing implies giving something up. The choice to read this conclusion implies that you did not read Chaucer, watch MTV, or take a walk in the park. This is what economists call opportunity cost, that is, the cost of the most attractive alternative to your choice (Buchanan 1969, vii). There is another, related, yet different view of cost. When a dilemma exists, getting more of one thing means getting less of another. Short of a technological change, these trade-offs are severe. They require us to choose, to sign on for more of "x" knowing that we will get less of "y." Politics of course enters the process. A society does not act as a whole, in unison, with equal costs and benefits for all. In the move to the single European market initiated in the mid-1980s, owners of capital—particularly mobile capital—were much more in favor of

136

freeing up capital controls and deregulating the regional market than were workers.

The creation of a European market raised questions about the social rights of market participants. One dilemma of constructing a European social policy centers on the relationship between national and European social policy regimes. As we observed, national policy regimes are quite strong, institutionally entrenched, and electorally powerful. As European social policy has developed, it has been by and large not at the expense of national social policy. The relationship is not zero-sum. It does not involve a tug-of-war between national and European social policy, an inch gained for Europe resulting in an inch lost for the member states. What is emerging instead is a multi-level polity in which multiple layers of political activity and responsibility are grafted together and intermingle (Marks 1992).

In a sense, European social policy addresses a different set of concerns compared to national policy. European social policy addresses itself to problems that arise at the European level. It deals with problems arising from people participating in the market in "other" European countries (Portuguese in Germany, Italians in the Netherlands and so forth). When international market failures exist, responses may most effectively be formulated at the international level.[1]

While a zero-sum relation may not exist, this does not mean that European social policy is simply an "add-on" to national-level policies. The existence of a European market, and European policies, may result in downward pressures on the social policy regimes in the member states. It is not so much that European social policies displace national policies, but that the growing transnational market makes for a much more competitive environment in which costly social regulations must be scrutinized at the national level. As Streeck (1997, 644) argues, European integration has increased the possibilities for cross-border mobility, both for people and commodities. This creates downward pressures on regulatory costs and makes it more difficult for labor to hold its own in national bargaining between employers and unions. National social policies, and even firm-level bargaining arrangements, may therefore suffer from European integration.

The second dilemma concerns the grounding of social policy. Do the foundations of European social policy lie in the market or in some universal conception of rights—citizenship rights, supranational rights, European rights? The evidence points to the importance of the market in generating and limiting the spread of rights. Ostner and Lewis (1995) identify the marketplace as one of the needles' eyes through which social policy must pass. As they put it:

> EU policy toward women seems to have reached the limits of what may be expected in the current framework, and any new proposals are likely to be

merely the unexpected or unintended byproducts of the increasingly complex politics of logrolling. The existing body of directives and rulings is sufficient to generate a continuing stream of important policy adaptations, but the two needles' eyes—the employment nexus and the constraints of member–state cultural and political diversity—greatly narrow the space for EU policymaking (Ostner and Lewis 1995, 193).

If some say it is true that European social policy is strongly tethered to the market, others go even further and argue that expansion of the European market creates strong downward pressures on the social and political bargains serving as the foundations of national welfare regimes. Thus the same powerful factor—the creation of the European market—stimulates the growth of European social policy at the same time that it erodes the bases of domestic regimes. Streeck (1997) has argued this position forcefully in his critical review of European social policy. Martin Rhodes (1995) has referred to this process as "subversive liberalism," a process by which international market integration eats away at the domestic bargains that have governed the linkages between the market and politics.

The EU has made only limited beginnings in social policy. Claims on behalf of a "social Europe" should not be exaggerated. In comparison to domestic welfare states, the European dimension is small, limited to the market, and strongly circumscribed by what states cannot do for themselves. Social rights are not inspired by basic rights of men and women that rest on a universal basis (natural law) or on membership in a political system, in the same way that all Germans, Belgians, and French are entitled to a certain set of rights and are bound by common responsibilities.

Against the background of the limited achievements of European social policy, critics have been numerous. Realists can argue that the states are still in control, still make the key decisions, and still hold the purse strings. Keynesians can argue that judged against the baseline of fiscally powerful national welfare states, with elaborate and expensive social policies, the EU's achievements are puny. And rights-based theorists can point out that virtually no social policy exists unless linked to market participation. If rights are to reflect membership in a participant political culture, rather than in the economy, then European social policy is all but nonexistent.

Despite the above criticisms, progress in social policy has taken place, it is significant, and it is likely to continue. The market is a powerful and pervasive institution. It is not just a technical device to facilitate economic exchange. As Fritz Scharpf has concluded, "There will hardly be any field of public policy for which it will not be possible to demonstrate a plausible connection to the guarantee of free movement of goods, persons, services, and capital" (Scharpf 1994, 6). Because of the practical implications of economic exchange, further social conflicts will doubtless emerge, resulting in pressures for further extensions of social policy at the European level.

A second set of dilemmas concerns democracy in the EU. The EU has often been criticized for not being democratic. This should not be surprising since the founders of the EU designed the institutions in such a way that final authority and legitimacy rested with national institutions. Also, we should keep in mind that the expansion of the regional market was seen by some—business organizations, holders of mobile capital—as a way of escaping national political controls. Yet, as the EU grew and the market became strong, people naturally asked to whom the actors and institutions were supposed to be responsible.

The separation between the regional market and national political systems is not necessarily bad for democracy. It is possible for us to imagine an integrated regional marketplace that is controlled by a decentralized system of nation-states. This is more or less what the founders of the EU envisioned. For Jean Monnet, the distinctive aspect of the European unity project, that which made an ideal possible, is that it dissociated both nationalism and the state from regional economic integration. That is, nations and nationalism, as well as the political institutions that defined the separate states, were to remain intact while the national economy would give way to a regional economy. As we have seen, the extension of the market to the regional level has resulted in the extension of property rights, freedom of movement, the application of laws of nondiscrimination, and limited social rights related to the market.

A negative side also exists. Multinational corporations operate more freely in their new transnational environment. People who own capital, particularly financial capital, can move it quickly, and with less constraints, than holders of other assets. In particular, workers still are primarily restricted to work inside their country of national citizenship, though they are legally allowed to migrate. In addition, regional integration has changed the balance of political forces that decide policy. Workers are less represented than capital at the regional level, and some national-level institutions such as centralized bargaining (between labor and capital) have been put under severe pressure.

The chapter on social policy contains a message for democracy also. Citizenship and democracy have always been thought of as closely related, if not inseparable from one another. A citizen is someone who is a member of a political community, and this community is constituted by the state. In the EU, citizenship is more a function of market participation. This departs significantly from traditional ideas and ideals of citizenship. A player in the market is not the same as a member of a *polis*. The two categories may overlap but they are also different. If market participation is crucial, then citizenship is contingent, that is, it depends on the vagaries of the market. To be put on firm ground, democracy must be guaranteed by the state. But the problem with extending traditional conceptions of citizenship to the European level is that a European state does not exist, at least not one that looks much like states at the national level. With the state, the market, and citizenship decoupled, the prospects for democracy are diminished.

Yet, there is much movement in Europe to strengthen its democratic institutions and practices. Democracy is an ongoing activity, a process that is continually contested in its new European space. The European Parliament is now directly elected, and all EU citizens can vote, regardless of the EU country in which they reside. Interest groups are directly represented in Brussels, and even sub-national regions have won representation. And as we have seen, the ECJ had laid down an elementary structure of rights on which the EU may build so as to extend social rights in different directions. Even if a catalogue of fundamental human rights will have to wait for another day, some progress has been made. So long as a European state remains weak, authority will rest with the member states, and this will discourage further progress in the growth of democratic institutions. Accountability, transparency, participation, and representation are important not only in their own right, but also because they are closely linked with the transfer of authority to the European level.

The third general area examined concerns external relations. External relations have traditionally implied conflict, controversy over national interests, and jealous concern about sovereignty. Thus, we expect the least amount of cooperation in external security relations. We can point to transatlantic tensions, the conflict in Yugoslavia, obstacles to the GATT trade negotiations, and charges of neocolonialism with regard to many less developed countries, especially the Lomé countries with which the EU is associated.

Whatever one thinks about the benefits and costs of the EU, it is hard to see it as "fortress Europe." A striking example of the external impact of the EU has to do with the introduction of the European currency (the Euro) in January of 1999. Within Europe, the Euro brings exchange rate stability and lowers uncertainty with regard to financial transactions. But what about the impact on the outside world? For those outside of Europe who hold assets in one of the member states, for example, a U.S. firm that owns a subsidiary of a corporation in the Netherlands, it will be easier to conduct business operations in the other member countries. However, there are some potentially conflictual areas also. The greater the strength of the Euro, the greater the threat to the dollar. This may manifest itself in changes in financial holdings as governments and private investors shift their assets out of dollars and into Euros. As the demand for Euros goes up, so too will pressure to revalue the Euro go up. One analyst, the former chairman of the Council of Economic Advisors (Feldstein 1997), has even argued that such monetary competition could lead to military conflict between the United States and the EU. While this is an unlikely scenario, the fact that a respected economist writes about it suggests that we consider it as one possibility.

What about the relationship between regional integration and global arrangements more generally? David Mitrany, both a visionary and a British pragmatist, was deeply pessimistic about regional unity in general and European unity in particular (see Mitrany 1930; 1963). In "Pan-Europa: A Hope or a Danger?," Mitrany saw regional unity and European imperialism as linked (1930). But the regionalism he criticized was based on Austrian Count Coudenhove-Kalergi's concept of a resurgent Europe in which culture, economy, and politics would be fused. The Count's project was to advance the mercantile interests of Europe as a whole, raising tariffs externally to the extent they were lowered internally, creating a protected market in Europe. He also aimed to save Western civilization and Christianity from barbarism—"The struggle for Pan-Europa is a struggle against barbarism" (Mitrany 1930, 471). By contrast, Europe's modern economic polity is firmly in the hands of an ascendant liberal elite that intends to profit through market competition rather than cartels, protection, and political influence.

In addition, Europe's modern political-economic-cultural formation is fractured. Politics, economics, and culture overlap but are not congruent. The market is transnational, regional, and even global. Identities are multiple (Marks and Haesly 1996; Risse 1999). They are attached to traditional nation-states as well as local units. There is hardly any worry that the primordial sentiment attached to the nation and for so long fused to the state, will shift to Brussels. In political terms, Europe is a multi-level, post-national polity with final authority still located in the constituent states. The European state, while it exists, is utterly defanged. It is small, has a budget less than 1.3 percent of the collective GDPs of the member states, and does not really engage in the traditional state's tax-and-spend activities. It is not a larger, more efficient version of France, Germany, and Italy. The institutions of the EU have deepened, but this deepening has not led to the creation of a superstate.

Finally, for good or ill, the EU has not made much headway with regard to common foreign and security policy. It is doubtful that the lack of progress is due to weak institutions. From European Political Cooperation in the 1970s, to the more extensive provisions regarding CFSP in the Maastricht and Amsterdam Treaties, Europe has developed the legal and institutional foundations for foreign policy cooperation. It is rather that the states making up the EU simply do not yet agree on what to do in their external relations. In democratic theory, state leaders are representatives of their national publics. It is their job to carry out policies reflecting the will of their publics. State sovereignty implies the right of national leaders to decide on what is in the interests of their country. Although the tension between state sovereignty and cooperative decisionmaking is an enduring one, in the area of foreign policy, states jealously guard their right to decide.

Writing a book organized around the concept of dilemmas creates a dilemma of its own. This is unavoidable. Viewing European integration through the lens of trade-offs means downplaying areas where cooperation and mutual reinforcement are characteristic. Completion of the free trade area and single market encouraged further integration, both economic and political. These positive couplings are part of the integration process also. Despite this, carrying out research for this book has confirmed the prevalence and staying power of dilemmas. The tensions between national and regional levels of social policy competence, between open and accountable democratic decisionmaking and expert problem solving, and between an inward-turning EU versus one that is fully engaged in broader global problems are deeply rooted and likely to endure in the decades ahead.

NOTES

1. An international market failure exists when a potentially productive international exchange does not occur due to inadequacy in either the policy or institutional framework. Such failures of exchange are not due to resource shortages, shortages in productive factors, or the absence of the desire for exchange. An individual may want to work in another country, there may be a job available, someone is willing to hire the foreign worker, and the resources to carry out the exchange may be fully adequate. But the institutional framework may discourage the exchange, for example, rules governing recognition may be vague, or social security provisions governing working in a foreign country may create obstacles.

REFERENCES

Buchanan, James M. 1969. *Cost and Choice: An Inquiry in Economic Theory*. Chicago: University of Chicago Press.

Feldstein, Martin. 1997. "EMU and International Conflict. *Foreign Affairs* 76, no. 6 (November/December):60–73.

Marks, Gary. 1992. "Structural Policy and Multilevel Governance in the EC." In *The State of the European Community*, vol. 2, edited by Alan W. Cafruny and Glenda G. Rosenthal. Boulder, Colo.: Lynne Rienner Publishers.

Marks, Gary, and Richard Haesly. 1996. "Thinking Through Territorial Identity in Europe with Reference to Some Evidence." Paper presented at the International Conference of Europeanists, Chicago, Ill.

Mitrany, David. 1930. "Pan-Europa: A Hope or a Danger?" *The Political Quarterly* 1, no. 4 (September-December): 457–478.

_____. 1963. "Delusions of Regional Unity." In *Limits and Problems of European Integration,* edited by B. Landheer. The Hague: Martinus Nijhoff.

Ostner, Ilona, and Jane Lewis. 1995. "Gender and the Evolution of European Social Policies." In *European Social Policy,* edited by Stephan Leibfried and Paul Pierson. Washington, D.C.: The Brookings Institution.

Rhodes, Martin. 1995. "Subversive Liberalism: Market Integration, Globalization and the European Welfare State." *Journal of European Public Policy* 2, no. 3: 384–406.

Risse, Thomas. 1999. "A Europeanization of Nation-State Identities?" To appear in *Europeanization and Domestic Change,* edited by Maria Green Cowles, James Caporaso, and Thomas Risse. Ithaca, N.Y.: Cornell University Press.

Scharpf, Fritz W. 1994. "Community and Autonomy: Multi-Level Policy-Making in the European Union." Working Paper, Robert Schuman Centre 94/1. Florence, Italy. European University Institute.

Streeck, Wolfgang. 1997. "Industrial Citizenship Under Regime Competition: The Case of the European Works Councils." *Journal of European Public Policy* 4, no. 4: 643–664.

Index